THE REDEMPTION OF KYLE PRESCOTT

CHRIS HONOWAY

Published by - Spines
ISBN: 979-8-89569-063-5

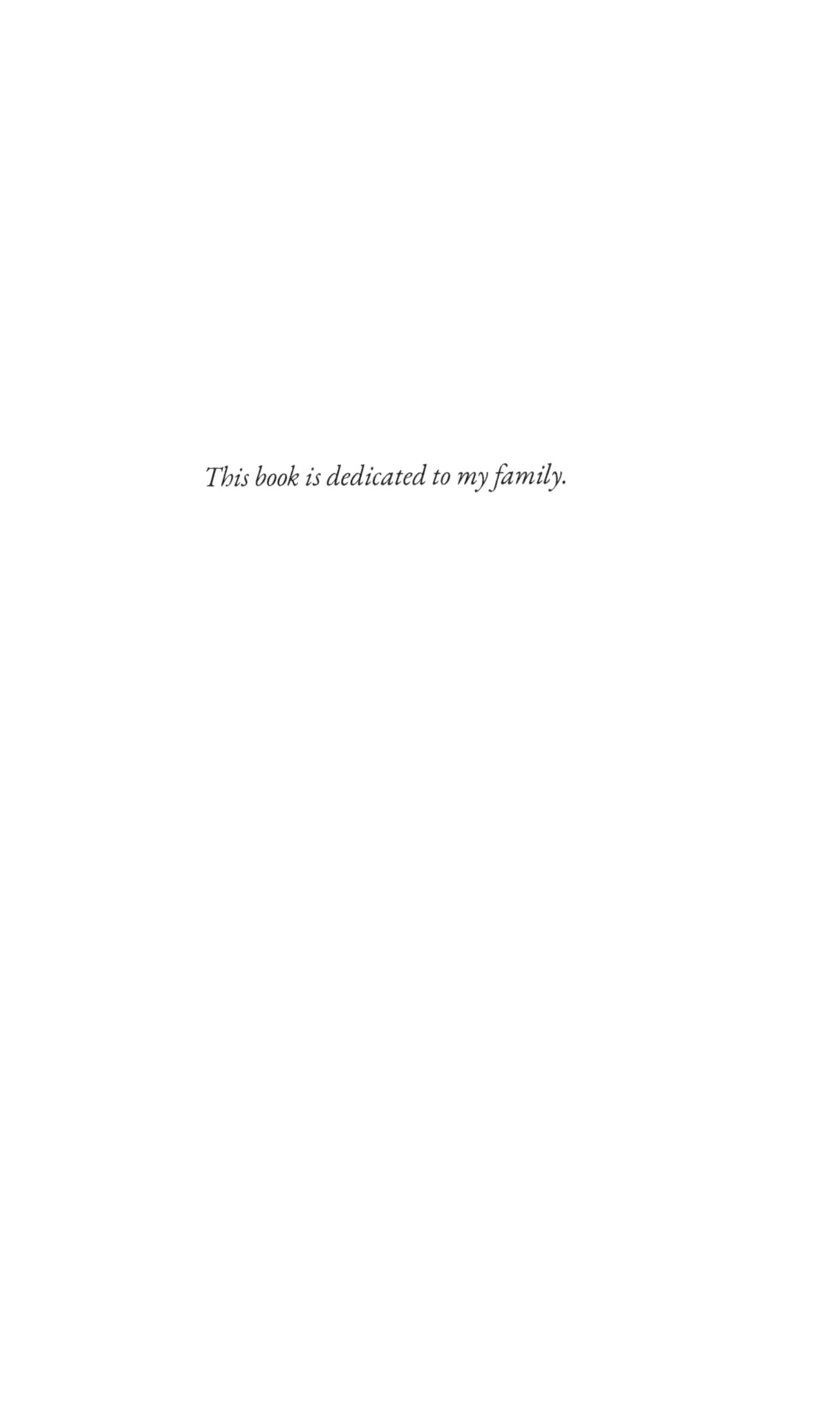

This book is dedicated to my family.

CONTENTS

Prologue — 9

1. If You Can Stand, You Can Play — 11
2. The Worst Day Of My Life — 16
3. Coldwater Blues — 24
4. Life Is Too Short To Say What If — 31
5. On Ice Assassin — 41
6. Time Capsule — 52
7. Out of Body Experience — 59
8. Bright Lights - Dark Past — 66
9. The Haunted Book — 73
10. Road Trip Revelations — 79
11. Get Dressed! — 88
12. Just Play Hockey — 97
13. Calgary Stampede — 103
14. Attracting Problems — 111
15. Showtime — 117
16. Families Matter — 122
17. The Winnipeg Warlords — 131
18. The Ghosts of the Olympia and Maple Leaf Gardens — 143

THE REDEMPTION OF
KYLE PRESCOTT

PROLOGUE

The blinking red light at the intersection seemed to be the only consistent element left in this deserted town. The metal clang of the flagpole rope was the loudest sound in the snow covered city centre. Banners reading "Go Kyle!" and "Believe" were plastered across Main Street, as the hometown hero, Kyle Prescott, was just moments away from the biggest game of his life. The townspeople watched his highlights play on TV screens in bars, diners and the comfort of their homes, anticipating the game taking place an ocean away.

Back home, Riverstone Bay practically belonged to the Prescotts; they were almost royalty. On that frigid morning, the whole town had shut down as the captivated locals held their breath, just like the rest of the world. The shared dream, once held by two brothers, now weighed heavily on Kyle's shoulders.

Growing up, Kyle Prescott was inseparable from his younger

brother, Connor. The pond near their home was their arena, their canvas where they created masterpieces on the ice.

For their age group, they were among the best, both displaying an overwhelming amount of competitiveness and skill. Connor was a natural goal scorer with Wayne Gretzky-like instincts, while Kyle, the speedy centreman, stuck to hockey's core values from many years ago. Their older sister, Stacy, a champion figure skater, filled the void left by their absentee parents. Her grace on the ice translated to her brothers' powerful yet flawless skating.

The Prescott Brothers' high school games became must-see events. Scouts, fans, and national media flocked to their modest arena, mesmerized by their raw talent and undisputed passion for the sport. Under the guidance of their intense coach, Darryl Johnston—a man who saw their potential when they were in grade school—the brothers led their team to three consecutive OFSAA Provincial Championships. For Kyle and Connor, the NHL was no longer an impossible dream; it seemed inevitable, something their little town took pride in. But life, as it often does, had other plans...

CHAPTER 1

IF YOU CAN STAND, YOU CAN PLAY

As I looked at the sea of people staring at me, I began to panic, but I reminded myself that I wasn't doing this alone—not this time, not anymore. After a couple of moments of silence, I could tell the crowd was becoming restless—or maybe that was just me overthinking everything. Regardless, thousands were waiting for me to share a few words about this unique, historic occasion.

So I breathed in the cold February air, looked at a beat-up spiral notebook, and began reading the words written by my brother several years ago. But I'm getting ahead of myself. Let me start my story much earlier.

For most people, New Year's is a time to reflect on the past year and look forward to the upcoming one. But in our hometown, we were more focused on what lay ahead in our hockey season—more specifically, the World Junior Championship. It didn't matter if you were eight or eighty-nine—everyone in Canada knew this tournament was more important than New Year's resolutions. Hell, it was even more important than college football in Alabama.

For those who don't know, the World Juniors involves the best young hockey players from around the world. Sometimes it's held in Canada, sometimes in the States, and sometimes even in Europe. That year, Stockholm, Sweden, was the host, and I was invited to represent my country along with three teammates from our hometown, Riverstone Bay. Not only were twenty-three of us competing for the red and white, but we were also fighting for our own hockey careers.

Scouts were watching every move we made, and one wrong move could end our dreams of becoming professional hockey players. That's a lot of pressure for a high school student, and this tournament wasn't as easy as we had initially imagined. We should have known better.

Hockey players from around the world keep getting better—they get bigger, and they get meaner. I'm not just talking about the Russians or Swedes, either. The Americans were there, and they were always tough. We got past them in the semifinal, but our starting goalie twisted his knee in the process. All that was left was the gold medal game against Finland.

Even though the tournament was held in Sweden, you wouldn't know it inside the loud arena, where booming chants and yells literally shook the entire place. The pro-Canadian crowd was like a pack of rabid dogs, outnumbering the Finnish fans three to one. Many had their faces painted red and white, and about a third were waving our flag from side to side, accompanied by the sound of air horns and bells. We all fed off that energy, and it's something I'll never forget. I'll also never forget how winded I was from being double-shifted the entire game.

We were in the third period with about a minute left, and the next goal would likely be the game-winner. We desperately needed to kill this penalty, but we were stuck in our zone. We'd been on the ice for about ninety seconds, and every breath felt like pins and needles as the cold arena air entered our lungs. I knew I had to get a whistle, or we'd be facing a long flight home as losers.

The Finnish point man faked a shot, then passed to his winger. He fired but hit the post. I skated toward the puck and lifted it as it caromed off the glass. I was sure it would leave the zone, but it didn't. The puck took a funny bounce off a glass partition and landed right back on the Finnish point man's stick. He took another shot, and it struck me square on the ankle. The puck deflected out of play. My adrenaline surged, distorting my sense of how bad my ankle was.

As expected, Finland called a timeout, which allowed us to get instructions from our coach. As I skated to the bench, thinking my shift was over, I couldn't have been more wrong. Coach stood at the gate, blocking my exit.

"Coach," I said in a weakened tone, "it's my ankle. I don't know if I can play."

Coach's stoic expression said it all, but, as usual, he had something to add: "If you can stand, you can play... we need you out there, kid." Then he tossed a bottle of water at me.

Still on the ice, I took a huge gulp of some much-needed water, but what I really needed was the team doctor.

"If you need me to play," I said, "I think I might—"

Coach cut me off. "I think you need to shut up." He then put it all in perspective. "This is what you've been talking about since you could talk. This is your life. This is all of our lives, our identity, and this is our game."

It seemed like Coach had hundreds of those John Wayne or Sylvester Stallone-type quotes in his mental arsenal—you know, the things nobody ever said in real life. But at that moment, he was right. This wasn't some Saturday morning open skate with my buddies.

This was the biggest moment of my life, and it was playing out in front of the whole world in real time. I thought about everyone counting on me: my brother Connor, who should have been playing but had a shoulder injury; my sister Stacy; my beautiful girlfriend, Julie; and everyone else watching back home.

If I could get through these twenty seconds, I thought my life would change for the better. The arena horn rang out, indicating that the timeout was over, and we slowly skated to the face-off. I knew how important this was. Everyone knew.

Besides, this is our game—not the Americans', and definitely not a bunch of pale blondes from Europe. The face-off was inside our zone as Finland was ready to put us away. I got closer to the face-off with intense pain.

Here we go, I thought, drenched sweater, ballooning ankle, and the whole world watching. Let's go.

The referee dropped the puck, and I lost the draw. The puck

went back to the Finnish point man, and he tried to pass it across the ice to the other defencemen.

That was a big mistake, and I stole the puck. My ankle slowed me down, so I passed it to my teammate, Phillips. He burned past two opponents to get into their zone, but he was running out of room. I crossed their blue line, with every stride more painful than the last. He passed it back to me, and without thinking, I fired, and the puck found its way into the net!

It wasn't the nicest-looking goal, but it was the most important. With only one second left, it was obvious that the game was over. We won. We just won the World Junior Championship! This was the greatest moment of my life, but everything would change in less than a year.

Winning it all was a big deal for us—for all of us. We came back from Europe as heroes. There were parades, TV interviews, the whole deal.

I'm not saying this was the 1972 Summit Series goal or the 1980 Miracle on Ice, but it was pretty close. In my mind, I became a made man, and the narrative of me being the next Steve Yzerman didn't help my humility, either. A lot of mistakes were made around the time I turned pro. The newspaper said I squandered a potential Hall of Fame career. TV said worse, and honestly, they were right. They both were. After being the MVP and gold medalist of the World Juniors, and playing in the NHL, how did I screw everything up so fast?

CHAPTER 2

THE WORST DAY OF MY LIFE

Almost ten months later, I re-injured my ankle early in my rookie season. I didn't think it was a big deal, so I went back home to regroup. Honestly, I was never one hundred percent after the World Juniors, so I needed some time to heal. For the next few weeks, I thought it would be the perfect time to be around family, spend time with friends, and get closer to my girlfriend, Julie Carter.

Julie had an aura that only movie stars had—thick, layered brown hair, high cheekbones, and a perfect jawline. She looked like Brooke Shields back when she did those designer jean commercials.

During my three years with Julie, I wasn't the best, or even a faithful, boyfriend. It was hard not to cheat back then, especially with women always around. I messed up sometimes, but I promised myself I'd stop soon. I was going to marry Julie one day.

The night before, when we were together in her room, I told her I had a surprise for her the following day, but she said it could wait until Monday. She was headed to Cochrane to see her cousins, but I didn't listen and the next day I got there before she left.

I was driving to her mom's house in a new Corvette I'd just bought! Thinking to myself, Wow, we did it. It was going to be our moment, our victory lap. She deserved this as much as I did—she was there for me at all my games, motivating me when I was too sick or too hurt to play. Without her, I wouldn't have accomplished anything. I wasn't worried about my little ankle injury; I assumed it would heal in a few weeks, and no one would even remember I was injured. All I cared about was spending time with her.

As I parked my car at the curb, I felt the excitement building. She walked down her long dirt driveway wearing blue jeans and a white T-shirt, a size too small, just to show off.

But my excitement deflated; something was wrong. Her face had no emotion at all. As she opened the door and got in the car, she dropped my flip phone on my lap.

"You forgot your phone," Julie said casually.

"Uh...thanks," I replied nervously. I was hoping she didn't find out about Tiffany, Amber, or Kelly.

I put the car in drive and headed to the city centre, but Julie didn't say anything, and she wasn't even looking at me. That was weird—she always had something to say. So, I stopped the car and asked her what the problem was.

"Kyle, I think we should cool it for a while."

I looked at her, shocked. "Cool it? What do you mean?"

"I think it means we're breaking up."

She continued, "I'm proud of everything you've done, and we had some great times together, but I've had enough."

This is bullshit, I thought. "Alright, who is it? Is it Lopez? He always said how much he liked you."

"Oh my gosh, Kyle, just stop!" Julie snapped.

Maybe it wasn't Lopez, but I couldn't take this loss. Backpedaling a bit, I said, "I was busy, you know, playing professional hockey—the thing I wanted to do since I was three."

Julie still wasn't looking at me; she just stared out the passenger window. Maybe I'd just said something that made things worse; I probably did. But that incredible chemistry we once had was gone, and I could tell she'd already made up her mind.

"That's my point, Kyle: you put hockey before everything in your life."

But what else is there? I thought to myself, but even I wasn't stupid enough to say that out loud.

"You being back for a few weeks with a new car and a couple of bucks in your pocket isn't going to change anything between us," she said, her voice frustrated and defeated.

"Change what?" I yelled. "I seriously don't know what your problem is!"

Then came the accusations.

"Where'd you meet Kelly? How long have you been messing around with that one?"

I didn't deny or own up to her claims of infidelity. Julie got out of the car; her perfect face was mixed with emotions.

"Goodbye, Kyle." She slammed the door. That was it. I just broke up with my girlfriend, so I floored it out of her life and headed to The Beer Store.

Julie dumping me didn't sit too well, but this wasn't going to ruin my plans for the weekend. She had the nerve to break up with me? I thought. I actually planned to leave the car for Julie, but then thought my brother and sister could use it instead.

Inside The Beer Store, I got a couple two-fours—almost fifty beers would be enough for the weekend. My brother was known to drink a little, so I figured we could catch up. God knows I hadn't had much time for him lately.

Just like old times, we played video games, but this time, we both drank quite a bit. After playing Super Nintendo for a couple of hours, the phone rang, and I answered.

"Hello?" I said.

"Prescott, we got a party at the water tower tonight. Let's go."

It was Luke McKay, my old teammate, known for throwing amazing parties!

"Who was that?" Connor asked as we kept playing NHL Hockey.

"It was McKay," I said. "He wants us to go to his party."

"I don't feel like it," Connor replied, scoring on me in the game.

Frustrated, I told him, "Let me tell you, little bro, getting to the next level isn't just about how well you can play."

Connor, still focused on the game, said, "I'm not worried about any of that extra shit Kyle."

I just scored on him and said, "What, are you too good to be around your teammates all of a sudden? Being with your team off the ice makes for a better team. Besides, this is getting kinda boring; this is the stuff we did when we were little kids. There's a party with my old teammates and your new ones, hot girls who idolize hockey players. Dude, we have to go!"

"How are we getting there?" Connor asked. "You've been drinking all day."

"Not a problem, little man," I said. "The party is just down the street, so it's no big deal."

Connor questioned me. "Little man? Alright, fine, let's go, but in case you haven't noticed, we're the same size now."

"Oh, so you want a shot at the champ?" I said, smiling as I playfully bear-hugged him.

"In your dreams, superstar," Connor fired back.

On the way to the party, a radio station was going over the scores from some games that night, and then they mentioned how Pittsburgh beat my team 7–1. They talked about how poorly we were playing so far and they even said how under-whelming my season had been. Connor, always the voice of reason, told me they were right.

That annoyed me a little, so I joked, "Yeah, I'd love to see you accomplish half of what I've done, but you won't. You'd prob-ably rather sit in some café reading poetry than play in the show."

Brothers argue all the time, but this one was worse than any argument we ever had.

Connor balled his right fist and lightly hit the inside of my door. "Kyle, I'm a year and a half younger, yet I've always been the better hockey player! And the funny part is, hockey's the only thing you care about, and I happen to hate it now!"

Maybe this was him standing up for himself after everything older brothers do while growing up. I didn't know, but this wasn't like him at all. Connor had this intense look on his face that I'd never seen before, and he continued his verbal onslaught.

"In five games, you have no points and are a minus-seven... Oh, and you're already injured... Way to go, next Steve Yzerman. In three years, you'll be dead broke and out of the league, and when it's all over, you're just gonna be some trivia question on a coffee cup!"

I've never... ever... seen him this upset! During this heated sibling rivalry, I wasn't paying attention to the road and was about to smack him. Then, I ran a red light, and a semi-truck broadsided the passenger door, flipping the car over three times. My brand-new Corvette landed upside down. My forehead was cut, but that was it.

Connor, on the other hand, wasn't so lucky. He was right there in front of me, and he was dead. This was bad, and it was all my fault. As I stood on the side of the road in total shock, the chill of the October night added to my insane shivering. I'm not sure if I stood there freezing for three minutes or forty—I guess I'll never know.

The next thing I remember was the distant sound of sirens. I wasn't sure if it was an ambulance or the police car that was going to take me to jail. All I could think of was how I wished I had been the one to die. Witnesses were pointing at me as they explained to the police what happened. Right before the cops walked up to me, I turned my head and saw the paramedics zipping my brother into a body bag and loading his lifeless body into the ambulance.

The ambulance slowly drove away without its sirens on. An officer walked up to me and flashed his light in my face.

"Are you injured?" he asked.

I didn't respond.

"Were you drinking?"

Again, I didn't respond. They'd find out soon enough that I had no business driving. By this point, I knew my life was over. No prison sentence or punishment could ever be worse than what I had just witnessed — nothing.

Sure enough, I was put in the back of a police car and taken to jail, and the news picked up the story fast. I was sitting in a holding cell, which smelled like overused disinfectant spray, but I could still smell the urine. It was cold inside that small concrete slab, and I had my arms tucked inside my shirt, still freezing, staring at the speakerphone mounted on the wall. It looked like an old payphone with metallic buttons, only without the receiver. I knew I had to make a few calls, and the first one was to Stacy.

There was no answer.

I hung up and dialled Coach next. He picked up on the first ring. "Yeah," he said, accepting the charges. My body was jittering as I said, 'Coach, it's me.' There was a long pause, and I waited for him to say anything.

Finally, he spoke, bluntly. "Kid, you gotta be a man for once in your life and deal with this." Then, all I heard was the dial tone. In that short amount of time, he gave me my next strategy for my new life. I tried calling Julie right after, but she didn't answer; she had to be at her cousin's by then.

I wasn't sure if she knew what had happened, but anyone who didn't know the sad news that night definitely knew by the morning. Everyone also knew it was my fault, and nobody had any sympathy for me. That dark cloud tormented me for so many years.

CHAPTER 3

COLDWATER BLUES

I'm sure plenty of people thought I was just going to kill myself. Well, I thought about it, but I knew God shows no mercy for that. Still, years after the accident, when I went to bed, I would ask Him to take me home. Maybe one day my town and family will forgive me. But after more than fifteen years, there's little to no evidence of that. Hell, I still haven't forgiven myself, so why should anyone else if I can't?

After my legal battles, I had nothing left. No money, no contact with my family, and no desire to ever play hockey again. All the attention after the World Juniors was absolutely the worst thing for me at nineteen. The winning goal, the accolades, the injury, and the accident causing death—that sequence of events changed the trajectory of my life.

I'll be honest: I wasn't doing anything to seek forgiveness or get any type of help; I just existed, doing my best to hide from the world. Some people reached out, some didn't, but I didn't make any effort to communicate with anyone. What would I say to them? I was embarrassed. Since the accident, I honestly never even set foot in my hometown. Facing all the people I let down was something I wasn't able to handle.

My toughness on the ice didn't seem to translate off it. The accident was something I still couldn't deal with—survivor's guilt, self-loathing, remorse? Call it what you want. I felt like a piece of shit. I spent more years than I'd like to admit just getting by with odd jobs—stocking shelves, painting fences, or working at a car wash. My skills were limited, and I wasn't making much money, but it was enough to cover rent and food, so fuck it. If I went back to school, what good would it do? I barely knew how to read when I graduated. One of the reasons I even passed was because of who I was. But now, ironically, who I am is getting me nowhere. But I knew I needed to do something more meaningful than washing cars at my age.

Years later, I noticed a local hockey rink was looking for someone to teach kids how to skate. Even though I thought I was done with hockey, I still needed it. But I was pretty sure I needed hockey more than hockey needed me.

So, I walked into the rink and suddenly realized how much I missed it—the sound of pucks hitting the boards and the plexiglass, even the smell of the Zamboni exhaust. Like an addict relapsing into an old vice, I was once again hooked. I inquired about the skating instructor job at the concession stand, and the man behind the counter lit up like a streetlight at dusk.

"You're looking to be an instructor?" he asked.

"Yeah," I replied, then quickly corrected myself. "I mean, yes. Yes, I do."

"How well can you skate?" he asked.

Without hesitation, I replied, "Well, I've been on skates before I knew how to talk and was trained by one of the best ice skaters in the world."

Kent nodded, handing me an application. "A background check will be run. So, have you ever been arrested?"

This question always came up when I was looking for work, and it was always the hardest part. He didn't know who I was, but I wasn't going to lie, so I came clean.

"I got in a car accident that caused a death when I was 19 years old."

Kent looked at me with a great deal of sympathy.

"Oh wow," he said softly.

"I'm Kyle Prescott. I played in the NHL, and the person who taught me how to skate was my sister, Stacy Prescott."

Kent looked at me, confused.

"She won silver in 1988," I added.

"Silver?" Kent asked, still puzzled.

"The silver medal! In the Calgary Olympics, for figure skating," I explained.

How does someone running an ice rink not know what the silver medal is?

Kent took a sip from his coffee and nodded. "Well, Kyle, we need an instructor. Classes start next week at three, so be here by 2:15."

That was it—I was hired. Who would have thought that just

walking into a local ice rink would be my first step toward my redemption?

The following week, I arrived early and knocked the rust off my skates. After about 20 minutes, I was skating as smooth as ever—maybe not as fast, but still good.

For almost two years, I watched these kids grow up and learn the same things I once did: the fundamentals of hard work, making new friends, and becoming hockey players. I'm pretty sure the legend Don Cherry coined the term The Canadian Way, which means playing tough, not dirty, and standing up for yourself and your teammates.

The little Tim-Bits' first steps onto the ice sometimes ended in immediate falls, but they were brave enough to continue, just to fall again, but still, they kept fighting. With each spill, they learned to find their balance, only to lose it again but move farther ahead the next time.

After each practice, parents told me how excited their kids were to see me each week, as we had coffee and discussed the little ones' development.

Teaching these kids gave me a purpose. I guided them through proper techniques: stopping, accelerating, and crossing over. But they taught me the most valuable lesson: perseverance.

Their determination to keep getting up, to dust the ice scrapings off their little mesh jerseys, was truly inspirational. We learned from each other valuable lessons in taking chances, succeeding, failing, and trying again—not giving up was our motto, our war cry.

Teaching the kids gave me the same feeling I had when I first learned to skate with Stacy. I felt reborn. Off the ice, one good habit led to another, and I even cut back on drinking.

I realized that without these lessons, I would have never been able to survive the next seven or eight months that were waiting for me. Thinking I had a decent thing going, Kent called me to talk about a few things. I was more than excited, because I had some ideas for next month's season that I wanted to run by him. When I arrived, Kent had his own ideas that he wanted to run by me.

"Kyle, I have good news and bad news."

"What's the bad news?" I asked.

"The lessons are cancelled for the season."

I should have asked him for the good news first. "Okay... what's the good news, then?"

"You still have a job here at the snack bar."

"The snack bar? That was the good news?" I asked.

"Well, yeah. So, do you want the job or not?"

Looking down, I kind of mumbled, "I'll take it."

That wasn't a great day, and it was very humbling for sure. Not giving up might have been my war cry but it looked like someone here gave up on me. To make things worse, it would have been Connor's birthday that day. When I took my walk home, I stopped at the variety store, realizing that cutting down on drinking wasn't gonna work for me at the moment, and I drank heavily—very heavily.

To celebrate Connor's birthday, I watched old home videos of him, and the shots of cheap vodka went down easier than I'd like to admit. Man, I can't remember the last time that I was this hammered. Even getting up from my couch was difficult.

Shit, I wasn't even able to go to the washroom to puke... I just lay on the couch, not being able to move. While I was vomiting on myself, I wondered if this was my post-accident rock bottom, and if it wasn't, I'd hate to see that day.

So, I passed out around three AM, and in the early afternoon, I was woken up by the sounds coming from my buddy's room. He was in the other room fooling around with his girlfriend, which kind of annoyed me—not because they woke me up, but because it made me jealous. Jealous because I hadn't gotten any in a while. Heading to the washroom to clean the chunks of shame off me, I asked myself, Why would any decent woman want anything to do with you? When I was the guest of honor at my own pity party, my phone rang. So I answered it, and it was the same kind of call I heard eighty or ninety times before.

"This is a collection agency, and we have called you several times to collect a debt from you, and this phone call will be recorded for training purposes."

So I quickly responded, "According to my attorney, this is a form of harassment, and it's against the law."

"Relax, kid, I was messing with ya; it's Coach Darryl Johnston."

Somewhat interested in hearing from Coach, my heart jumped a few more beats.

"Coach," I said with a hint of excitement, "what's going on?"

"We need you to come back home."

"For what exactly?"

"To try out for us. I'll explain it all when I come out to see ya; you're in Coldwater, right?"

A bit shocked, I said, "Yeah, how'd you know that?"

"I'll see ya in a couple of days, kid."

"Yeah, but I didn't even say I was gonna try out yet."

Coach then said to me in a calm tone of voice, "Yes, you are." Then he hung up before I could ask how he even got my phone number.

It wasn't a mystery that Coach hadn't had a winning hockey team in years, and the arena he was coaching in was falling apart; come to think of it, so was the town. This was the same town I once called home. The same coach who handpicked me for the World Juniors. On the night of the accident, he must've felt like he'd lost two kids. He was the closest thing I had to a dad—I'd never even met my father.

CHAPTER 4

LIFE IS TOO SHORT TO SAY WHAT IF

A couple of days later, I spent my day off at the rink, taking shots at an empty net—a perk of selling Skittles at the snack bar. With only half the rink lights on, the ice had a darkened, eerie, cinematic aesthetic. Skating required no thought for me; every turn, hop, pivot, stop, and push made me feel free, like I could fly. My lungs burned; my upper thighs were sore, but I remained in control as I coasted between the face-off circles and fired a shot.

Top left corner!

It hit the bar inside the net, making that sweet, dull sound of iron—all while imagining Bob Cole's legendary voice yell, "Scooores! Prrrrrrrrescott!" with the pretend crowd cheering! All of a sudden, my childlike fantasy of winning the Stanley Cup came to a halt when I heard a familiar voice.

"You know it's a lot harder when there's a goalie in front of that cage, right?" It was Coach, and the sound of his voice always put me in a sense of uncertainty. I hadn't seen him since Connor's funeral, where police escorts prevented me from speaking to anyone.

Coach was standing at the players' bench, and I skated toward him. Like a thousand times before, he handed me a bottle of water. I took a sip and said, "I don't know if I'm ready to go back to all of it."

Then Coach knocked the water bottle out of my hand and impatiently said, "Cut the bullshit, Kyle; get your things and let's go back home."

He wasn't messing around and skipped his usual motivational speech.

I wasn't in the mood for tough love, so I said, "Home... yeah, I'm sure everyone will be thrilled to see me."

Coach chuckled softly and said, "I know you, I know the town, and believe it or not, you're both in the same spot—wounded, abandoned, and a little desperate."

"Coach, I'm not sure I want to hear any of this."

Then Coach climbed over the boards, took my hockey stick, found a puck close to us, and slowly stick-handled as he continued to speak. "Kyle, hockey isn't that complicated. There are only three things a hockey player needs to know:

You fight battles against others...

you fight battles within yourself...

and you face the truth even when you don't want to."

He paused and had an intense look in his eyes that burned right through my soul.

"This is one of those times when you must face the truth. Riverstone Bay isn't doing very well, and we need something to stop the bleeding."

At that moment, I looked away from him, which really pissed him off.

"Look at me when I'm talking to you, kid; you owe it to yourself to come back and finish what you didn't even start! More importantly, you owe it to the town. You're a big part of its past, and yes, I'm blaming you for the position that it's in right now!"

Standing there, helpless and ashamed, like a puppy caught pissing on a Persian rug, I stuttered, saying 'umm' and 'uh' a few times. But Coach cut me off. 'The game is still calling you, and you still need it. Life is too short to say what if.' What could I say after that? He handed me my bus ticket, and a couple of days later, I was on my way back to Riverstone Bay.

I later found out that the idea of me coming back came from the team's interim owner, Colton Ryerson. Colton's father was too sick and weak to handle the day-to-day responsibilities of overseeing the team, but he still had enough energy to remind Colton that he was a screw-up.

So, technically, if his old man wanted to classify his son as a failure, I guess history was on his side. Colton, at only twenty-four, already had quite the legal résumé: soliciting prostitution, drug possession, drunk driving, and domestic violence—you name it, he could do it all!He was less than a year away from getting his father's trust fund, but he wasn't going to see a nickel unless he cleaned up his act and significantly improved his dad's hockey club. With so much on the line, Colton was trying anything to get the team back on track. Coach felt the pressure put on him by the management, and now that pressure was also put on me.

Coming back to town was something I knew I had to do sooner or later, and the latter came sooner than I thought. But still, being watched by any type of hockey team at this point was a huge blessing.

But I was still afraid of facing my estranged family and trying out for a team with some players almost half my age. The ride took a couple of hours, and as I stepped off the bus with my old equipment bag and hockey stick in tow, I saw the familiar buildings that had been a big part of my childhood. The buildings were still there, but they no longer had signs that read "Now Open." Instead, those signs were replaced with things that said, "For Lease" or "Going Out of Business."

The comic book shop, the arcade, and the hardware store were just memories. It wasn't all gone though. The Beer Store was still around—but of course it was. This place had become a drinking town with a hockey problem. It felt like I had stepped into an alternate universe, one I would always be linked to. Walking past the boarded-up exteriors of yesterday, I was haunted by memories while living in this bleak present.

Not long after the car accident, the town's steel mill closed, leaving many out of work and putting a lot of people through hard times. The only thing this town could still identify with was hockey. The youth programs brought in a little bit of money, but the minor league hockey team The Riverstone Bay Wranglers, was supposed to be the town's main draw. Unfortunately, they hadn't been good for almost ten years.

A culture of constant hockey failures and economic hardship had become the norm for the entire city. Being in this epicentre of disappointment made me realize that I might have bitten off more than I could chew.

The tryouts would happen soon, so once I settled at the motel the team provided, I didn't waste any time training. The very first thing I liked to do to get back into shape was run. I'd get to plyometrics and weightlifting later. Getting my wind back was first before I could do anything more advanced, so the treadmill at the motel would do.

I didn't want to overdo it on the first day, so I selected a moderate pace that I would stick to for about 50 or 60 minutes, and it wasn't as bad as I thought it would be. In fact, I was feeling pretty good 30 minutes in, but just then, I turned my head toward one of the televisions in the fitness centre, and damned if it wasn't a news report on the Wranglers.

Son of a bitch.

The first day I came back to town, everyone knew about it. There was one other person in the fitness centre, barely doing anything on some exercise bike, who looked at the TV and then quickly looked at me.

Don't get me wrong, I was happy I wasn't selling Kit Kats at a snack bar, but man, I never missed this unwanted attention. I left the fitness centre to avoid the awkwardness and decided to finish my workout by running outdoors, but it wasn't as easy as running on a treadmill. Honestly, I wasn't ready for that yet. The hills and the rugged outdoor terrain were a thousand times tougher than the motel's Nordic Track. But that was only half of it. When I jogged past more old familiar places, more haunting memories kept coming back.

Mocking me.

Intense glimpses of Connor's accident burned inside my brain, along with the day I first kissed Julie and the argument I had with Connor right before the truck hit us. I knew this would happen if I ever came back here. But I didn't think that it would be this bad so soon.

The next morning, I began my day with another outdoor run attempt, and in the middle of my workout, I noticed more unwanted attention with my photo on the town's newspaper front page, the headline reading, "Prescott Back in Town; Can He Save Us?" I stopped what I was doing and began reading. Colton Ryerson was interviewed in the article, and his demeanour in the story was that of someone who knows what second chances are all about.

The article was a total PR move, an attempt to make himself look good, and I'm sure this was his whole idea in the first place. They over-sensationalized all the attributes that made this story appetizing to the reader: "A fallen star who was finally given a chance at redemption. A story of hope, for him and the people directly affected the day Connor Prescott died."

I wanted to avoid all this attention so early on, but I knew it would come eventually. My sister had to know about it by now, and I knew I needed to see her soon, but I was still afraid to face her. I'm sure Ryerson loved the attention, but it meant nothing unless I proved myself on the ice.

After finishing my workout, I took a walk to the sports bar on the corner of First and Maple Street called The Corner. I wanted to keep a low profile, so I quickly found a spot at a bar table, grabbed a menu, and held it up over my face before anyone could notice me.

When I looked at the place, I observed that nothing really changed with their decorations. A couple of changes were made here and there, but it was pretty much the same theme with the hockey vibe going on. But I did notice a few subtle changes.

There was a memorial for Connor and more photos of Stacy's figure skating accomplishments by the same jukebox with the same Van Halen songs from the '70s. Those photos of my siblings conveniently replaced the picture of myself, which was a huge black-and-white photo of me raising my arms right after World Juniors.

I've been erased.

Someone obviously didn't like me here. Hopefully, I could get a beer and a sandwich minus the saliva. The bar wasn't packed, but it was steady for a Monday. The kitchen wasn't that far from me, and I heard bar employees complaining about all the things that bar employees complain about. One of the voices I heard was a familiar one; I knew it was her. Once again, I put my menu over my face, concealing my identity as the woman I loved more than anyone impatiently asked me what I wanted to eat.

She spoke in my direction, "Yeah, what's it gonna be?" I put down my laminated shield and said, "What do you have on tap?"

Julie gave me one of those looks so cold that the middle of January would be jealous. This lasted for no more than ten seconds but felt like ten minutes. Just then, an impatient bar patron began shouting in her direction.

"What's it gonna take to get a cosmopolitan around here?"

Julie turned her head in disdain. "It'll take a sex change, buddy," she yelled.

Sean, a bar regular, laughed at the well-dressed man. "You might wanna lower your standards around here, bud."

Julie didn't look too entertained with Sean. "Sean, fuck off." She then quickly walked away from the bar back into the kitchen area reserved for staff.

My cover was blown. Bar patrons looked and whispered as they noticed me. Since everyone knew it was me, I decided to get my money's worth. I walked through the kitchen, past the bar employees and cooks, to follow her. Outside, I found Julie in the alley where the busboys dumped the trash, she was lighting up a cigarette.

As she took her first hit, I was in a trance, captivated by her matured looks: a tight body, brown hair with hints of blonde, and subtle facial lines, yet still incredibly stunning. Suddenly, I snapped out of it when she practically bit my head off.

She shouted, "You have a lot of nerve coming here like this!"

Trying to be funny, I said, "I know, I think the line cook is pissed at me for walking through the kitchen."

Julie didn't think that was funny, even though it kinda was.

This time, I wasn't joking around and said, "You probably

heard that I was invited to camp. You know this is my last chance."

Julie's knowledge of hockey was on par with anyone, man or woman, and she told me, "It probably is your last shot, especially since no other team would touch you."

Looking down at the dirty ground in the alley, I told her something she wasn't ready for. "When I said that this was my last chance, I wasn't talking about hockey, Julie."

She didn't know what to say, so I continued, "I'll be staying at the Edward Bronson Motel down the street for a little bit; my room number is 248."

She took another drag from her Du Maurier and told me, "You've done a good job staying away from us all these years, and I was hoping you'd keep it that way." She threw her cigarette on the ground and walked back to work. When she suggested staying away from us, she meant herself—likely my sister—and definitely our son, Derrick, who was already in prep school.

I didn't know much about him, except for two things we shared: we were both hockey players, and neither of us had ever met our dads. Standing by the dumpsters alone, I picked up the still-lit cigarette, looked at it, and remembered I had quit two days before. So I tossed it back on the ground and said out loud, "I think she took that rather well."

Yeah, it was true. I never met Derrick, but I tried. I wrote him letters and sent him birthday cards. Who knows if he ever got them? Coming back here was more complicated than just playing hockey, and I was having a hard time figuring out what would be more difficult: the battles against my opponents, or with myself, or facing the truth.

To play hockey well into your thirties, you have no choice but to work twice as hard as someone that's, say, twenty; you just have to. Skating was out of the question because the old rink was closed for renovations. So, to train, I continued running outdoors and began weightlifting and did plyometrics, which is just a fancy term for jumping exercises.

The next few weeks went by, and I lost almost fifteen pounds by cutting down on beer, drinking more water, eating less bread, and focusing on lean foods like grilled chicken, broccoli, and salmon.

With all the training, I was close to the shape I was in when I won the gold medal. Executing this wasn't enjoyable, but it was empowering. As for talking to my sister Stacy, I didn't even attempt to go to the old house, but at the same time, she didn't reach out to me either.

CHAPTER 5

ON ICE ASSASSIN

The first day of tryouts finally came, and I was really, really nervous. The last time I played against skilled hockey players was when I was nineteen, and I was about to find out how good I still was—or how bad I'd gotten. The training camp invited forty players, with about twenty-four spots available. So, figure it out—twenty-four were going to stay, and sixteen were guaranteed nothing.

I walked into the players' entrance and was bombarded with news reporters, photographers, and TV crews. Walking past the multiple reporters, I could hear remarks about me being spoken in news-speak. They said things like, "Prescott, a former hockey prodigy, lost it all after a tragic turn of events..." I quickly escaped the crowd and entered the dressing room. Coach was already there, talking to one of his assistants. He was decked out in a blue CCM skate suit, baseball cap, and hockey skates. He tossed me a white practice jersey. "You better be ready," he said and headed out of the dressing room.

His words repeated in my mind, like a saying from an old TV show. You better be ready! But this time, his one-liner seemed a little more forced than usual. Why? I realized it was because Sports Wire was here. They were the biggest sports station in the country. About twenty cameras were all over the arena, with full access to the ice, the bench, the locker room, and, for all I knew, the washroom too.

The locker room door opened, and in walked interim owner Colton Ryerson. The muffled voices of news reporters became clearer once that door opened, and I heard more manufactured reporting: "Prescott spent several years living in obscurity until today, where he returns to an opportunity to once again play hockey." Colton, with perfect hair and pop-star stubble, stood confident in a tight blue suit. He was talking to one of the reporters, smiling and answering questions by just nodding and saying things like "absolutely" and "no doubt about it."

With his fake politician smile and spearmint gum chewing, you could tell he was loving all of this. Colton and his stocky assistant, Dale Palmer, entered the locker room. Colton, demanding attention, shouted, "I'm happier than a pig in shit right now!"

Colton continued with his bravado. "In about a year, this trust fund will be as good as mine!" We all looked up, then went back to whatever we were doing. He wasn't done bragging. "All this attention is gonna make us a lock for National Hockey Day!"

Colton looked at me and nodded, which was a little weird.

"And everyone thinks I'm a bad guy," he said to himself. Dale chimed in to kiss his ass, "You'll be remembered as the man who saved this town!"

"Absolutely," said Colton. Then Ryerson and Dale walked out of the locker room.

"National Hockey Day?" one of the players asked.

"The thing with an outdoor NHL game? That's some serious shit," someone else added.

Another player trying out was Cody Larson—a big guy, probably 6'3" and around the age of twenty-one or twenty-two—finished taping his stick. He slowly put it down, looked at me, and said, "So that's why they asked you here... for some TV show? What a joke."

Damn, he actually might have had a point. From an outsider's perspective, it definitely seemed like the owner was using me. But if he had his own motives for inviting me here, then so be it. I just had to make the best of this opportunity because I had my own reasons for coming back. Besides, the talk of National Hockey Day potentially coming here would be a big deal for Riverstone Bay.

Each year, a small town is selected to host several winter activities, such as pond hockey tournaments, skating lessons, ice sculpture exhibits, and a televised professional outdoor game. It's big-time money. This could be the driving force for the hockey club to get a brand-new arena and possibly save the town. Everyone had their own story and personal motives—the owners, the coaches, the other players, and me. Needless to say, things were about to unravel as tryouts began.

The attention I was getting from Sports Wire put a bounty on my head. Now a bunch of players wanted to make a name for themselves in front of all the cameras. Walking down the tunnel to the ice, I just knew I was ready. After a few laps around the rink, with my slightly oversized jersey flapping in the wind, my aching joints took the day off, so I felt great! During warm-ups, Coach had a couple more one-liners and told the assistants to remove the pucks from the ice. He loudly said, "No pucks today, boys; I'm gonna find out who's out of shape really quick. Five of you are going home today."

Coach pointed at a few of us. "You, you, and you line up at the goal line."

One of the three asked to line up was me. Coach explained that he wanted to see us take a full lap around the rink at the sound of his whistle. Back when I used to play for Coach in my high school days, I was the fastest skater on his team, but that was a long time ago. Standing on the thin red line, the butterflies were in full effect, and we crouched with knees bent in our ready positions. I remembered how much I hated these drills. I was always more nervous during these times compared to important moments in the game.

The whistle blew, and we were off! I started off slow but quickly caught up to the other two. I was still behind the younger skaters until we made our turns around the corners; that's where I really gained speed, crossing over my aging legs as fast as I could. My burst of speed was good enough for second. In my prime, I would have smoked both of those guys, but finishing second wasn't terrible.

For the next two hours, Coach skated us hard. He sure found out who was in shape and who wasn't. But I hung in there with the others trying out, along with the guys already guaranteed a spot on the team. As promised, five players were given bus tickets home—and I wasn't one of them. With all that being said, I still thought my first day was average at best. Maybe I was putting extra pressure on myself, but could you blame me? If I made this club, I wanted it to be because I actually deserved a spot—not to be some storyline on a contrived TV show. Having been off the ice for almost a month, I was rusty, and I'm pretty sure everyone could tell I wasn't the fastest anymore.

That afternoon, I hoped to regain my top speed, but like many things in life, once it's gone, there's no getting it back. I had to adapt to my body's limitations and hockey's newer style—a tall order. After practice, Ricky Lawton, a rookie from Livonia, Michigan, offered some encouraging words: "You can still skate," he said, nodding. "That makes a kid like me want to step it up."

Lawton was far and away the best player on the ice. I could tell he had more maturity than I had when I was his age. He was the type of hard-working player that every team needed if they wanted to win a championship. Despite his maturity, and blazing speed, something about him confused me.

Before we got onto the ice that day, I noticed Lawton on his phone. Whoever was on the other line with him had him shaken up. So I asked him, "Hey, is being away from home working out okay?"

"Yeah, I mean, you know, hey, where's a good place to eat

around here?" His vague answer and sudden subject change weren't very reassuring.

Brad Drexell, a seven-year veteran, overheard us and invited Rick and me out: 'Meet us at The Corner!' Most of the guys agreed to go, including the Newfie guys and *Les Boys de Québec*, who stuck together due to language barriers. But when *The Corner* was mentioned, my appetite quickly vanished.

I was afraid Julie would be there, and I didn't want to see her at the moment. But I recalled what I told Connor—being with your team off the ice makes better teams. Still, I didn't want to look like I was stalking my ex-girlfriend at her work. But I was in luck that day; someone else was working the bar shift that afternoon, so I avoided that stalker stigma for at least one day.

When it was time to order, someone acted like a ten-year-old soon enough. Cody Larson walked in, obviously high, drunk, or both, and his presence was known the second he entered. He picked up right where he left off in the locker room with his colour commentary, "Hey, never-was, where all the cameramen at?" He kept harassing me, and I was sick of him—his attitude, and even that ridiculous foot-long beard. Everything about him screamed "tool."

So, I got out of my seat, walked up to him, and said, "Does that long beard make up for something below the belt?" A few guys laughed but quickly shut up when Cody gave them a dirty look. I wasn't sure if he was going to do something or not, but I didn't want to get arrested again. It was time to leave.

When I walked past him, I bumped my shoulder into Cody, saying, "I'll see ya on the ice, tough guy." I walked out of the bar, wondering if he'd follow me to fight, but he didn't. Good. That bought me some time to figure out how I was going to take on a guy who was a few inches taller and actually enjoyed fighting.

Maybe what I did wasn't very smart, but I never claimed to be a rocket scientist. But I knew that if I put Larson in his place, it would remove any doubt that I belonged on this team. The walk back to my motel room was brief. During that short walk, I kept telling myself that facing Cody was another giant task I had to conquer during my visit home. That alone was a lot; I still had to resolve my issues with Julie and reconnect with my sister.

When I got back to my motel room, I tried to sleep but didn't get much. Part of the reason was that people next door had a constant flow of visitors throughout the night, probably for something illegal. The other reason I stayed awake was how tense I was for the next day of camp. When I finally did get some sleep, I had a recurring nightmare that had already played in my mind almost fifty times.

It was Connor's funeral service in the same old arena we used for training camp. The arena was at full capacity, with students from kindergarten to college and all the townspeople—all crying. They even had a bagpipe quartet play "Amazing Grace." But this time, the dream had one little twist: the person inside the coffin wasn't Connor. It was me.

Trying to make sense of it all, I realized I had no time to analyze what I'd just experienced because I was already running late for my real-life burial by Cody Larson's cold hands. By now, everyone on the team knew what had happened at The Corner, and I was sure they expected to see something between Cody and me.

When I got into the dressing room, Coach told me to put on a black practice jersey to play against players wearing red in a five-on-five scrimmage.

Wouldn't you know it? I'd be playing against Larson, who was wearing a red uniform! Well, someone wanted to see something, didn't they?

We lined up for the face-off, and one of the assistant coaches had the duty of dropping the puck. I won the draw and tried to focus on the play while keeping my eye on Cody. I had some room and hoped our defencemen would pass it to me, but he fired it into their zone, so I quickly skated toward the puck. Cody was there to greet me with a hit against the glass. The pads absorbed most of the hit, and I was still able to dig the puck out of the boards and pass it to Lawton, who buried it in the net.

That was enough for that shift, and we headed to the bench for a line change. Now that I had settled my nerves with an assist, I told myself to take one shift at a time.

A few minutes went by, and we made a change with no stoppage of play. I hopped the boards and received a pass right on my tape, and I was in the clear; it was just me and the backup goalie, Ryan Haywood. You only have a few seconds to decide what to do on a breakaway, and I waited for the goalie to make a move. He went down, and I shot it over his blocker, but it hit the crossbar.

The clang of iron and rubber echoed throughout the old arena, and as the puck found its way into the neutral zone, I skated to catch up to the play. Out of nowhere, Cody jabbed me in the stomach with the butt end of his stick. The wind was knocked out of me as I fell to the ice, gasping for air. Somehow, I got up and was close enough to the bench to get off the ice. As I sat, trying to get my breath with my head down, I could hear the other team celebrate as Cody scored.

Tie game.

Cody skated by my bench with a big smile, saying, "You're gonna love seeing that on TV!"

Now it was time to get him back, and I had a few minutes to strategize what I was gonna do next.

A couple of minutes later, I was able to breathe for my next shift, but the lines got messed up, and I knew exactly what was going to happen. I'd be out there for a minute or so, and Cody would be on the ice right at the end of my shift when I'd be more winded than him. So I conserved my energy as much as possible for the next thirty or forty seconds, just waiting for him to come out.

Finally, he did, and he received a pass, so I went after him and hit him at open ice; he fell, but so did I. Cody got up a little quicker than I did, and he got into position to score, and right when he was about to shoot, I stole the puck and passed it to Blake Shedden, and we were off for another scoring chance.

It was a two-on-one, and I could hear ice being carved behind me. I knew it was him; I received the pass from Shedden, and I had no time to fool around and aimlessly fired, scoring! But now, I was bracing myself for impact, and sure enough, he shoved me into the boards. No damage was done, but it was more of an insult than anything. I was on the ice for well over 90 seconds and was pretty tired, but I knew I had to stand up for myself. I slashed his ankle, and Cody turned around. We both dropped our gloves.

It was time.

Of course, Cody was doing the whole deal—taking off his elbow pads, raising his arms, and pointing his fists at me. So I did the same for a few seconds, mocking him, but then I had to stop with the foreplay and get into it. Everything seemed to slow down, and all I could hear was my rapid heartbeat and quickening breath. I hit him in the jaw, but it didn't faze him. Then he hit me pretty good, and I felt it even with my adrenaline. He got me again, and I felt that one too. I knew if I didn't do anything, I'd get seriously hurt. So I grabbed both of his arms, struggling to keep him wrapped up, hoping someone would stop the fight, but nobody did. I wasn't going to be able to hold him forever, so I let go of his left arm to pop him again with a left to his eye, and then, finally, the fight was broken up.

The players on both benches were pounding their sticks on the boards, yelling with excitement. Exhausted and thinking this beef was finally squashed, I hoped we could move on without any more of this Monday night wrestling shit.

Wrong. It wasn't over.

On the very next shift, Cody had more for me. As soon as he hit the ice, he was looking for me like a predator. The puck was in the corner, and I was tangled up with someone, trying to dig it out when Cody came charging toward me—stick and elbow up, feet off the ice—aiming right for the kill shot. If he connected, there's no telling what would've happened to me.

At the last second, I moved out of the way; he hit the glass, and you could instantly hear a scream so chilling that even an Eskimo would have gotten hypothermia. He was hurt bad. It wasn't life-threatening or anything, so honestly, as bad as this sounds, I didn't care.

I reminded myself how much of a prick he'd been since I met him. The fact was, he would've kept bullying me unless I did something about it—and with a little luck on my side for once, he took himself out. Medics had to stretcher him off, and it was official: the big, tough "future NHLer" Cody Larson would not be a Riverstone Bay Wrangler. It's not like I ever fancied myself to be some assassin on the ice, but now people are gonna make a big deal out of this, whether I liked it or not.

Chapter 6

Time Capsule

That afternoon, I took another walk around town, still in shock from the incident. I wanted to see my sister more than ever, so I decided to go to the old house. As I moved closer, the anticipation of seeing her for the first time in years was building as high as the fire being set down the street. The scent of hickory and burnt leaves consumed my senses as I realized I was only about fifty metres away from the place I once called home.

As I approached, I got distracted by a lawn service crew finishing up their work. When I reached the door, I turned and looked at the manicured lawn and playfully shouted at one of the landscapers.

"It looks good, but not as good as my brother and I once did it," I said.

"You're Kyle Prescott. You don't remember me, do you?"

Puzzled, I stood there with a blank look on my face.

"I'm Mitch Landon. We had shop class in grade eight."

This kind of thing happened a lot. Everyone knew me, but I rarely remembered most of my classmates. But I did have a prepared line for these situations.

"Yeah, I remember you. Ya kidding, hey!" That was my response, and it usually worked—but not this time.

"It's alright," Mitch said, looking down nervously. "I was really shy back then, so nobody remembered me."

There was an awkward silence. Then he continued, "You're back in town, eh? I read about you trying out for the Wranglers."

These situations weren't the most comfortable for me—when people know your life story, and I can't remember a thing about them. Hell, I'd already forgotten this guy's name. So I changed the subject.

"My sister isn't expecting me. I was gonna surprise her. She's here, right?"

The landscaper put down the weed whacker and thought for a moment.

"She won't be back for a while."

"A while?" I asked.

"Yeah, she's busy coaching in Europe with some figure skaters... She won't be back for a couple of weeks."

So, I kept the conversation going.

"A couple of weeks, eh?" The awkward moments kept adding up, and I couldn't take it. Luckily, the other landscaper called him over, saying they needed to move on to the next house.

"Well, hey, I gotta get going. Good luck, Kyle," Mitch said.

With a smile, I replied, "If I make the club, I'll leave a couple of tickets at will call."

The truck drove off, and now was my chance to get inside. As I anticipated, the door was locked. So, naturally, I broke in. It's not like I smashed a window or something, but I had to be resourceful to get past the dead-bolted doors and sliding glass windows somehow.

When I used to get locked out here, I'd climb the backyard tree to get to my room's unlocked window. So that's exactly what I did that time too; I scaled the tree, pulled myself through the window, and fell on the floor.

When I stood up in my old room, it finally sunk in that I was back. Taking a long look around, I realized nothing at all had changed. It was as if I were standing in a time capsule. Posters of Doug Gilmour and Wendel Clark were still hanging where they had years ago. Even my bed wasn't made, but Connor's bed was flawless—but of course, it was. I mean, he was the perfect brother.

The Super Nintendo still had NHL Hockey in it, bringing back memories of Connor and me, consuming too much Mountain Dew and junk food, playing for hours. For old time's sake, I turned on the game and the CD player beside it.

Everything still worked, but when the music started playing, it was the one thing in the room that wasn't the same. The song was The Cure's *Pictures of You*. Nothing against that band, but I wasn't a big fan of The Cure. My sister loved them, though. It was a deeply emotional song about losing someone and holding onto whatever memories you had left. This told me Stacy must come in here from time to time—and that she's still heartbroken.

With the calming music playing, I started the video game, and it was as if time stood still. Back then, those were some of the best moments of my life, and it took me all this time to realize nothing now would be as good or as pure as those days.

Though this room was frozen in time, playing this game alone as a grown man wouldn't bring back my youth. So I shut off the game. Next, I rummaged through a dresser drawer, looking at old hockey cards, homework, and I even found a drawing Connor had made of us playing hockey.

He titled it *My Best Friend*. Wow. Some friend I was, especially since his last moment on Earth was spent in an argument with me, fuelled by jealousy. The song was still playing, and, being a little more mature now, I could appreciate how beautiful and fitting it was for everything I'd just experienced in that room. Mixed feelings made me question if this was going to help me heal. The chilling presence of memories was all around me, and I turned off the CD player and got out of my room.

Before leaving, I went downstairs to look around the family room. As I entered the room, the aroma of cinnamon candles was still present, setting off more memories of all the good times shared here. In every corner, I could instantly recall birthdays, Christmas, New Year's—you name it. Those great memories made me feel even worse. It's hard to explain, but it was like I'd already lived this moment a hundred times.

After spending time in the old house, I needed a drink—or ten—so I headed to The Corner. By now, the buzz of my return had worn off, and I was a little less reluctant about being in public. I walked in and took a seat at the bar. The place was slow, and a nearby customer had left a ten on the table. Being a little bored, I looked at his bill: two Lakeports for $9.50. The server's name on the check read "Julie."

That cheap bum left her a fifty-cent tip, so I reached into my old denim jacket and put down a few toonies. My attempt to anonymously tip Julie failed when she walked out of the kitchen and caught me in the act. She swiped the cash, put it in the register, then filled a mug of beer and set it in front of me.

"We're even," she said boldly.

There was a moment of silence as I took a sip from the mug. Before I could mention that lipstick was on the glass, Julie blurted, "Heard you've lost a step in your speed."

I shrugged, telling her she wasn't wrong. Then I asked if she'd heard anything else. I had a feeling she had. She picked up an empty fry basket from the bar table, tossed it in the sink, and said, "You know this isn't over with Larson, right?"

"No, I don't know," I replied, taking another sip from the dirty glass.

Julie then gave me one of her scouting reports, just like she used to during my high school days.

"If you make the final roster, Winnipeg has Blaine Larson— Cody's older brother. He's already blaming you for injuring Cody."

My drink was almost empty, but before I could ask for another, Julie checked her phone, then grabbed her purse.

"My shift's over," she said, clocking out before heading toward the door.

I quickly followed. She looked annoyed, loudly exhaling and rolling her eyes, but I didn't care.

I tried to ease the tension with a joke. "I read about a prison breakout. Apparently, the convict swore to track down all the gorgeous brunette bartenders."

Her quick wit was still as sharp as a Bauer TUUK blade. Without missing a beat, she replied, "Congrats on learning to read, Kyle."

She finally slowed her speed-walking, letting her guard down. Then I said, "Last I heard, you were in France doing fashion photography."

Julie scoffed, saying, "It was actually Montréal. But, as you know, sometimes things don't go as planned."

"So here we are," I said. "Both of us, walking the same streets we did as kids."

Julie smiled, looking at me. "I know, right? It's kinda crazy."

"No, it's life," I replied.

We were the only two walking in the middle of the street in silence, as I took in more of the boarded-up facades of our town. Looking at the out-of-business comic book shop and ice cream store, it felt like they were sadly staring back at me. It's life, I thought to myself.

Once I noticed that we were headed toward her mother's house, I said, "Back home with Mom, eh?"

"Yeah, for a little bit," Julie replied. "It's the only way I can save up for our place." She was referring to her and Derrick, who we could hear talking with some friends down the long dirt driveway.

Julie stopped me from getting closer, saying, "This isn't the right time yet. But he has a game I want you to watch in a few days."

She then thanked me for walking her home.

"Anytime," I said.

Looking down, she said, "Get some rest for Detroit. You'll need it."

Julie shuffled toward her mom's house, and I stood there, admiring everything about her.

Chapter 7

Out of Body Experience

We headed to Detroit the next day on a bus older than me—which says a lot. Our exhibition game would be my first organized match-up in almost twenty years, televised live for everyone back home to see. The day was finally here. It was only a few minutes before we were going on the ice, and I could already hear the Detroit crowd cheering loudly.

Inside the small visitor's area, which smelled like a sewer, a few of the players, like Drexell and Smyth, were talking, but the immature jokes ended the second Coach walked into the room. He looked around the room and he began. "For some of you, this could be your last chance to prove why you belong with this club."

For effect, he power-spitted his chewing tobacco in the large circular garbage can that every locker room seems to have. Coach went on, "This is not just some exhibition game that doesn't mean anything."

Our weirdo starting goalie, Julian Richards, mumbled to himself, It's not some throwaway game up in Rochester, either.

Coach heard that remark and was pissed. "Richards, that's the main reason you're stuck with the rest of us and not with the Dallas Stars! Haywood, you're starting!" Coach exhaled deeply and continued, "Every time you go on that damn ice, it matters! I don't want to see any of you take it easy out there, and if you do, I swear to God you'll be back home digging ditches or selling Doritos at a snack bar!

He looked right at me when he said that.

"We all know you're up against the best team in the league. Don't make any mistakes either because if you do, they will embarrass you bad. Lawton, Prescott, and Drexell, you start."

Coach's speeches, though cheesy as ever, were still as real as they could get. We got up and exited the dressing room. I was walking through the narrow tunnel that led to the ice surface, and the closer I got to the ice, the louder the arena's acoustics got with the crowd noise and the rock music over the speakers, which was louder than any metal concert I'd been to.

One by one, we stepped onto the surface to take our warm-up laps. When it was my turn to hit the ice, I immediately took some quick strides to gain speed like Wayne Gretzky used to do. The crowd was against us, but I took pride in being the bad guy on the visiting team; it was our job to shut them up! The game was only moments away, and I still couldn't believe this was happening.

The cheering, the booing, the smoke from the pyro, and the

loud music of the arena anthem, *Rock and Roll (Part 2)*, felt almost like an out-of-body experience. The goosebumps on my arms didn't go away until the national anthems were over.

When *O Canada* and *The Star-Spangled Banner* finished, I crossed myself, put my helmet back on, and was as tense as ever. The old organ music of *Charge* played as we lined up for the draw. A player from Detroit faced off against me; I blocked out his trash talk and tried to get my head in the game, but it wasn't easy. My nerves were short-circuiting; it felt like a panic attack was about to happen right there on the ice.

It was the same kind of feeling you'd get when you prepared for a big speech in school and froze when it was time to deliver. As my excitement turned to fear, I channeled my emotions to focus on the game.

Here we go, I thought. Inside enemy lines, don't mess up, stand out tonight. Let's go.

The puck dropped, and I won the draw. Our defenceman, Dubois, gained control and fed it to me, but my nerves suddenly took over instead of being channeled properly. I fired a shot from eighty feet away, and the puck bounced off the goalie's pads. Lawton raced into the Detroit zone, snatched the puck, and snapped it past the tendie in just eleven seconds. The crowd was quiet, except for a few Wrangler fans' air horns and a handful of Rick's Livonia Stevenson High School buddies. Then the public announcer addressed the crowd in a monotone voice.

"Wranglers' goal, scored by number 19, Ricky Lawton. Assisted by number 93, Kyle Prescott. Time, nineteen forty-nine."

The public announcer was no Paul Morris or Bud Lynch, but he got the point across.

The PA announcement of my lucky assist boosted my confidence, and I played well for most of the game. In the second, I made a big hit that set up Lawton's breakaway goal. Then in the third period, we were still up 2-0, thinking we could just keep the pressure on and let them bleed out. None of that happened; they owned us, scoring two quick goals to tie it up, and before we knew what the Hell happened, they almost scored again!

We only had ten seconds left, and we wanted to win this damn game. The face-off was in the Detroit zone, and it was myself, Lawton, and Shedden on offence. Coach decided to replace our goalie with an extra skater, giving us a one-man advantage for these closing moments. We lined up against some massive players from Detroit, and they had this cocky look about them as we were about to take the face-off. Then, Coach called a timeout, and as we skated toward the bench, I thought Coach probably wanted to give us a rest before we finished the game. But he had another idea, and he took me off the ice and replaced me with Brandon Snyder.

When I climbed the boards to sit on the bench, Coach tapped me on the shoulder and told me, "You did great tonight, kid." I sat on the bench, thinking, If I did so great, why aren't I still on the ice? Going from being forced to play with a fractured ankle in World Juniors to being replaced in a minor league exhibition game was hard to swallow. The puck was finally dropped, with ten seconds left, nine seconds left, Lawton and Snyder spread out and passed the puck to each other; five seconds left, the defenceman, like a quarterback, passed it to the open man Snyder, and he shot the puck towards the Detroit net-minder and scored right before the buzzer sounded.

The game ended in a 3-2 win, so Coach's decision to replace me was the right one. But even though we won, this victory didn't make me feel too great about myself. Why would it? We still had players who dressed for this game who'd be sent home, and I could be one of them, handed a bus ticket back to Coldwater. Not being asked to play at the end was a reminder that nothing in sports is guaranteed. The mortality of my hockey career was staring me in the face, along with my fading confidence.

We got back from Detroit the next day, and the first episode of Front and Centre aired that night. Watching it alone at my place, I had to admit—it was done well. They had all the drama binge-watchers love. They covered topics like the town's dedicated hockey tradition and its desperate situation, with narration about the economic struggles people were facing—something the working-class viewers could easily relate to.

Was this an interesting show?

Yes, it was.

Did the show intertwine the importance of hockey in a small town searching for hope?

Yes, it did.

Did I enjoy watching it?

No, I hated it!

It literally hit home a little closer than I wanted. They had footage of me walking away from my old house. I had no clue that they even filmed that! They showed a clip of me skating a bit slower than the other players, and a part where Cody Larson crushed me into the boards.

That didn't bother me that much, only because they showed me doing a couple things that I did well on the ice. But the part that really bothered me was that damn narrator with his thick, deep voice talking about the car accident. They didn't stop there, either. Set to sappy, dramatic piano music, they interviewed old teammates and teachers, who talked about where they were when they found out about the crash.

They even had my son, Derrick, on the show! He didn't say too much about me. He was too busy talking about his future hockey career. He said he knows about me, and that damn narrator went on to say, "Derrick knows about his Prescott blood-lines, but is focused on starting his own legacy of being a Carter."

Overall, the show didn't make me look too good, but my biggest concern was the remainder of the exhibition season. I knew that if I wanted a spot on this club, I'd have to convince Coach—and hockey would have to mean more to me than life itself.

But just like when I was eighteen, hockey was, once again, my life. We played a couple of exhibition games at home, including one against Halifax, where we secured a solid win. I felt like I played my best that night, despite no points; Coach had me focused on shutting down their top line and last season's leading scorer. Against Cincinnati, though, we ended up with a forget-table loss. Then, we traveled to Quebec. One of Les Boys, Pierre Dubois, like Lawton did in Detroit, Dubois tore it up in front of his hometown crowd, scoring two goals. I managed to score one of my own and get three assists—all I really had to do was feed the puck to Lawton, who padded my stats by scoring almost at will. I felt strong and confident, even with my diminished speed, and was sure my performance had earned me a spot on the team.

A few days later, the final roster was posted, but things didn't go exactly as I planned. Looking at the roster pinned to the bulletin board, I saw that I was not one of the forwards on the list. I was devastated; there had to have been some kind of mistake. An assistant coach told me that Coach wanted to see me in his office right away. Coach let me in and got straight to the point. He said, "I'm sorry, but you're not quick enough to play for us."

I thought, Alright, this is it; I'm done.

Coach took a sip of his coffee, then put down his mug and continued, "You're not quick enough to play as a forward. You're going on defence."

"Defence?" I shouted. "But I never played defence before!" He really didn't have to convince me or anything because what choice did I have? This would be a bit of a learning curve, but a prerequisite of being a defenceman was being able to mix it up in front of our net and be a strong skater; speed was preferred but not vital, so I thought maybe this would work. When I got up from the chair in the office, I said, "All right, I think I can do it."

Coach gave me that familiar look of positive affirmation, the one he'd given me countless times before, and predictably said, "I know you can do it kid."

CHAPTER 8

BRIGHT LIGHTS - DARK PAST

After Coach was done with me, Colton Ryerson called me into his office to discuss a TV interview I had to do. When I entered I took a look around—I noticed how ridiculous his office was. It had arcade games, a punching bag, a basketball net, and he even had an oil painting of himself hung up behind his desk. All that was missing was a giant train set. I regained my focus and questioned him.

"My interview?" I asked, surprised.

Colton glanced up from his desk, where he was casually rolling a joint. "That's right," he said with a smile. "Your interview is in sixty minutes. But don't worry, babe; after all that hard work getting into shape, you look great. You barely have a double chin now!"

All I could think about was how much I didn't like this guy, but I had to keep reminding myself that he was the one with the elaborate plan to exploit me—to make this hockey club a success and save the town.

Once we arrived, there were about ten people, including myself, inside the little TV studio. Ryerson was trying to feel important, standing next to a guy wearing a scarf, who I assumed was the director or producer. Then, someone with a walkie-talkie took me to where a makeup person touched me up. While sitting there, I wondered what everyone would think when they eventually saw this. Being interviewed was nothing new to me, but it's not like I ever got comfortable in front of the camera. With all these lights and uptight assholes all over the place, it was hard to concentrate.

There were so many things that could go wrong:

What if I stutter?
What if I mumble?
What if I say something stupid?
What if I look hungover?
What if I am hungover?

Just then, I remembered what Coach said: *Life is too short to say what if.* But what if this interview sucks?

After the makeup made me look halfway decent, they clipped one of those little microphones on my collar, even though they already had that long mic resting above me. Then, before I knew it, the guy in a scarf holding a nine-dollar coffee was the one asking me the questions.

"Quiet on set!" he yelled. The interrogation began. Oh man,

there were a lot of questions. After almost an hour, I figured most of what they asked me would get cut by the video editors. I spent a good amount of time talking about how many kids from this town made it to the NHL, competed in the Winter Olympics, or went on to big-time American universities.

Not too much later, I noticed the directors and producers checking their phones, looking bored. Maybe they'd heard this kind of story a hundred times—small hockey communities, billet parents hosting players for decades, 7 AM practices, and pond hockey masterpieces. Maybe they thought it was becoming a trope. Trope or not, Riverstone Bay was proud of its identity, and that pride was real.

The director had other ideas, though. He stopped us in our tracks and yelled, "All right, cut. Let's take five." Before I could get up to go to the washroom, the makeup team did whatever they thought was necessary to conceal my age. Not too far from me, someone in his fifties was talking to Ryerson and the guy with the scarf, and he said words to the effect that it was time to move on from the hockey-town cliché and start asking the real questions.

Oh, they did, too. They asked me everything! I opened up to people I either didn't like, know, or trust, and I had to keep reminding myself that this was part of my job now. But knowing how the media works, I had no idea how they were going to spin this part of my story. When the story would air, it will be the first time people hear me talk about what happened the night of the accident.

Stripped of my armour of CCM pads and left alone in front

of the lights, *I felt vulnerable-naked-exposed to the judgments of everyone.* It was overwhelming. Telling my story was cathartic, but I couldn't fight off the *anxiety* gnawing at me or its impact on those I still care about; and that's the truth.

After the Sports Wire interviews, skating, and dealing with the owner, I barely had enough time to sleep. But still, I couldn't complain; quite a few weeks earlier, I was on a friend's couch, throwing up on myself. The contract I signed was for one year, and after taxes, I was making about $900 a week. That's not the most you can make in the minors, but it wasn't the lowest, either. Except for my time in the NHL, this was the most money I had made as a full-grown adult. Now that I was going to be staying in town for a while, I could finally check out of The Edward Bronson Motel.

As I packed up my belongings, I noticed my next-door neighbours were moving out, too. The police were kind enough to help with their move, driving them to their new home and carefully packing up their chemistry set in boxes.

For my next spot, I'd be rooming with Julian Richards, the starting goalie—our weird starting goalie. I forgot how old Richards was; I think he was 29 or 30. Richards played sparingly in the NHL for about five years until he found his way to minor league purgatory, with the rest of us. Goalies do get typecast as being a bit odd, and Richards fell into that weirdo category because he was kinda random and would say whatever was on his mind, no matter how stupid it was. But that didn't bother me. I could tell I could trust him, and that's all that mattered.

The regular season would begin in two days, giving me plenty of time to get settled into my new apartment. Finally, I found the courage to visit Connor. This was something I had never done until now, and for some reason, I thought this was the perfect moment.

Connor's well-kept grave was directly below my point of view; the wind picked up and stung my eyes. As I looked down at the grey and black granite, I stood still, not knowing what to say, but a safe bet would be to pray. After saying *The Lord's Prayer,* I noticed a bracelet sitting next to the headstone. The bracelet was a gift from Stacy to Connor.

The day he received that present, Connor and I walked to the video store to grab junk food, rent a movie and pick up a video game. It was the fall, and it got dark out of nowhere. We were already twenty minutes late when two older kids began to follow us. Everyone in town knew about the Prescott Brothers; and some were jealous. Before we knew it, the two older kids ran up and tackled us, trying to steal our belongings. We fought back the best we could, but they were too big. Right when things were getting really bad, Stacy, already looking for us, pulled up in her Chevy Blazer. She saved us from a severe beating. Connor got a bloody nose, and I took a hit to the head. It would have been much worse if she hadn't chased them off with the baseball bat she kept in her back seat. That night, she expressed guilt about not being there sooner. After that flashback, I was left with an uneasy feeling inside me, knowing that wasn't the right time to get the answers I was searching for.

At the next practice, we were greeted by a new player who had just been sent down from the Dallas Stars. His name was Garret Marshall. He was sent to work on his attitude and improve his conditioning. However, it didn't take long to notice he had a lot of work to do. He barely tried during the skating drills, saying things like, "This is bullshit," and, "Why am I here with these guys?" It was obvious he wasn't happy to be in the minors with us, and I wasn't the only one who noticed. His attitude created bad vibes between him and the rest of the team.

During the five-on-five scrimmages, Snyder and I took turns embarrassing Marshall, intercepting his aimless passes, and we constantly stripped the puck from him. He was lazy, likely relying too much on connections rather than actual talent. After the gruelling practice, I was heading toward the dressing room when Coach stopped me to say how well I had adapted to playing defense, and that I had shown enough to make the second line. Marshall heard this and "accidentally" bumped into me when we got to the locker room. Inside the locker room, I sat at my usual spot and untied my skates. Marshall sat down next to me.

"So," he said, his voice overloaded with sarcasm, "you made the second line on this clown show? Wow, you should be proud."

But I didn't take the bait; I didn't see the point. Everyone on the team already hated this guy, and Coach saw all of this go down, but for some reason, he didn't say anything. All of it was anticlimactic, if you think about it. There was no big fight or pull-apart or Coach throwing a giant Gatorade cooler across the room. Coach's calm demeanour was less entertaining, but we later learned he made a call to Dallas and told them Marshall wasn't welcome here, either. Dallas ended up trading Marshall's rights to another team that year; as far as we were concerned, Garret Marshall was someone else's problem.

CHAPTER 9

THE HAUNTED BOOK

A day later, Julie called and reminded me to meet her at the arena for Derrick's game. As I walked in, I noticed new teachers, old teachers, and current students mingling and enjoying themselves at the rink. The trumpets and snare drums added to the excitement of the cheering crowd, but none of that could compete with Julie's yells as she cheered Derrick's team on.

Growing up, there were always one or two hockey parents who went a little too far, and now, Julie was one of them. I waded through the people in the crowded bleachers. I couldn't see her at first, but I didn't need to—her high-pitched voice sliced through the noise, making her easy to find.

The teams were already doing their stretching and skating drills when I finally sat next to Julie. As I watched their warm-ups, I noticed something about Derrick. It was the way he skated.

He skated exactly how Connor and I did, with long strides carving the ice, leaving that satisfying crunching sound just a little bit louder than the others, and those crisp, smooth crossovers were so effortless that Paul Coffey would be impressed—probably making him want a skating lesson from Derrick. I mentioned how well Derrick could skate to Julie, and she said, in a matter-of-fact tone, "Well, he learned from the same person you learned from."

She was, of course, talking about my sister Stacy, the champion figure skater. Derrick's game started, and while watching, so many thoughts entered my mind: *my career was almost over before it even started, and now I was watching my son's hockey career begin.* Incredible.

The similarities between Derrick, Connor, and me didn't end with the way he skated, either. It was also the way he played. His skills were close to the guys already in the show. There was no question that he was the best player on the ice, kind of like how my brother and I were at his age.

But still, he did share a trait that I have that Connor lacked: intensity. That attribute could be a great asset or an enemy within. Derrick took a stupid penalty by being baited into pushing someone into the net. The crowd loved it, but that put his team in a bad spot. Julie was furious and said a few colourful words to herself.

"Are you really that mad at the ref? That was a dumb penalty," I said, while tilting my head.

"No kidding," Julie said, her voice raised with frustration. "I'm mad at Derrick."

As his team was killing the penalty, we avoided drops of water from the leaking ceiling.

"It's a part of its charm," I said.

A few drops of water found their way into the hot chocolate she was drinking.

"Oh yeah, especially when the health department shuts this place down. It's real charming."

The visiting team moved the puck like seasoned professionals and quickly scored a power-play goal. Derrick exited the penalty box and lined up to take the face-off. Julie said to me, "That team against us has the best rink in the league and one of the best training facilities in Ontario."

Derrick won the face-off and quickly got open as I replied, "That new stuff has its purpose, but honestly, it's just another gimmick."

Julie politely interrupted me.

"Shut up, Kyle."

Then Derrick got a pass before the blue line and split the defence exactly like Mario Lemieux in 1989; he then put the puck between the goalie's pads, scoring. Julie jumped up and cheered. Then I said, "See, love for this game and hard work beats sports science if you want it bad enough."

Julie smiled and lightly punched me on the shoulder. "Yeah, but this town needed a new barn like 20 years ago."

The rest of the game went by as Julie and I talked about nothing important. I could tell that the two of us were making a comeback, but I didn't want to look like I was trying too hard that night. I didn't want to say a single word whenever Derrick was on the ice because she was too busy yelling, probably doing a better job of coaching than the actual coach. Derrick scored another goal, and they won 3-1.

The fans got up from the stands, and I held my right ear. Julie looked at me with that concerned look that she always used to give me.

"What's the matter?" she asked.

"Oh, nothing," I said. "I just lost hearing in my right ear because of all your damn yelling tonight!"

"Oh, sorry," Julie said.

I laughed a little. "No, you're not."

"You'll be fine," she said. "Come on, follow me."

When it was time for parents to meet the players outside, Julie and I couldn't find Derrick at first. Then I spotted him from a distance, surrounded by friends.

This would be my first time speaking to him, and I had no clue what he would say; I was scared. But instead of feeling like I was in some reality show meeting my estranged son, it actually felt like watching the beginning of an after-school special about a troubled kid.

He was smoking pot and drinking with a couple of girls who were cheering him on during the game. Julie, full of anger, told the girls to leave. Derrick brushed this off, much like I probably would have at his age, and he got in the car with the two fans.

But right before he left, I made eye contact with him for the first time and told him to be safe.

Derrick just mumbled something like, "Yeah, alright," or words to that effect, and they left.

Julie explained how he's been out of control for a while and how his grades were slipping. From my perspective, these things were normal, and I told her that.

Then she blindsided me, saying, "Yeah, that's normal for you. Look how you ended up." She immediately tried to cover her tracks. "Kyle, I mean..." she began, but the words never came out. Julie didn't have to cover it up because she was right. But still, words hurt, and so does facing the truth sometimes. Pretending that it didn't bother me, I told her, "Hey, the season starts tomorrow with a road trip, so I have something I need to do."

"Let me drop you off, at least," Julie offered. "No, I'm alright. I'll see you after the trip."

What she said did hurt my feelings, but there was another reason I didn't want a ride home from her. There was something about Derrick that I needed to figure out. After the game, Julie and I went our separate ways, and I headed back to the old house. Entering the same way I did the other day, I got back inside my old room and looked into Connor's dresser again, but this time, I did a more thorough search. *Where is it!* I thought.

I dug through the old homework assignments and graded term papers, and after a few minutes of looking, I found a beat-up spiral notebook—but this wasn't his math homework.

These were years' worth of journal entries, revealing thoughts and feelings that nobody else knew about. Back then, I never paid attention to that stuff; I just thought his artsy, sensitive writing was a waste of time and let him have his privacy. But privacy be damned, after Derrick's game, I had to face the truth: there was no guarantee I'd get the answers I wanted, but the book I was holding might help.

I took the notebook and headed back to my apartment down the empty street. For some reason, I knew that once I read this book, I would be opening things that I might never be able to close again. Prying into these secrets could have a haunting impact on me, but there was no turning back. That night, I didn't read it. I wasn't ready. There would be plenty of time to read during the road trip tomorrow.

CHAPTER 10
ROAD TRIP REVELATIONS

We boarded our modest bus to kick off our road trip to Rochester, London, and Hamilton—in that order. The long drive would give me hours to read the notebook. Randomly flipping through the tattered pages, I read the following from Connor's journal:

December 2nd, 2004

Coach told me due to the stacked roster, only one Prescott could make the cut for Team Canada at the IIHF World Junior Championship. He picked me, saying I was "the better fit"

I don't buy it.

Yeah, I score more than Kyle and, well, I'm a smarter player than him too, but still, he's more valu-

able. He has this modern-day warrior spirit— he's fearless.

He'd risk everything—his body, well-being, even life—for hockey. Would I? No way. Kyle once told me, "Risking permanent injury or death for something you love isn't stupid or tragic...it's heroic." But he doesn't realize how sad that really is. I worry about his future when hockey is over. I really do. I feel sorry for him.

Kyle not getting selected would devastate him, so I'll come up with something because I'm not going to play in the stupid tournament. I don't love hockey as much as like Kyle does, so he can have my spot. Besides, Kyle doesn't love Julie as much as I love Julie!

Unbelievable, I thought as I kept reading.

Coach won't make the announcement until next Monday. That gives me time to figure out how to get out of this. Then we both get what we want: Kyle advances from round to round—and girl to girl in Europe—while I tell Julie how we're meant to be.

Trying to get in the middle of Kyle and Julie sounds pretty selfish, but he took her from me in the first place—or at least that's how I see it. Trying to justify this will get me nowhere. Those two are about to run their course anyway.

Then I'll be officially able to move in, so the least I could do was give Kyle my spot in the tournament—a type *of peace offering. No matter what happens, sometimes you get a chance at redemption, and this is my backward, messed-up way of doing it.*

A couple of days later, Connor slid into the boards and was out for six weeks. He either fabricated a shoulder injury or deliberately got hurt just to skip the tournament and be with Julie.

Reading that entry was disturbing. It wasn't explained in the book how bad his injury really was. But his plan worked; he always got the big picture better than I did. Like a chess player, he sacrificed his spot on Team Canada—his pawn—to take the queen. Connor believed I stole Julie from him in the first place, and he internalized that. But I never knew I did that—maybe I should have; I don't know. So who's really in the wrong here? Maybe all of us—I'm not sure. But now, with these road trip revelations, I've got a lot more on my plate than before.

Oh, and the journal entries weren't done, either. In graphic detail, Connor gave a play-by-play of how close they were in our bedroom. They secretly messed around any chance they could, including when I was in Sweden and even when I was in the NHL. This made me throw up in my mouth a little, especially now that there's a chance Derrick might not be my son. That's right—I might not be a deadbeat dad after all.

It all made sense, too. I was a lefty, and they both shot right-handed, along with those two being more skilled than me at their ages. We had three games in four days, and this was killing my focus. There was no way I was going to read any more of that haunted book. Suddenly, Drexell tossed me a beer, and I slammed it. Feeling a little better considering what I had just read, I said, "Gimme another, will ya?"

We weren't playing today, so screw it. Coach was already passed out, so he didn't know how much we were drinking. As we enjoyed the sights of cornfields for over two hundred kilometres, we continued drinking as Lawton broke down Rochester's strengths and weaknesses. Pretending to pay attention to Lawton's scouting report was easy; I simply nodded and said, "Uh-huh," like thirty-seven times. But how could I focus, knowing I'd been lied to for almost two decades? So, I drank seven beers in about an hour. I just wanted to sleep before we reached American customs.

After barely avoiding the rubber glove treatment at the border, we finally got to our hotel. Because of the morning practice, we didn't have much time to sleep. Sleep wasn't in the question that night anyway—not a second! How could I? For all those years, I thought I was the only one making big mistakes. Maybe Connor didn't think he messed up, or maybe he never had the right moment to come clean with me, but Julie had nothing but time.

When it was time to play, we weren't ready. In the first period, I was in front of the goal crease, tying up a forward from Rochester. Their defenceman fired a shot, and the puck hit my stick, deflecting it into the top corner of our own net. Coach was pissed, and he yanked me off the ice.

The rest of the game wasn't any better; we were flatter than piss on a pan, giving the puck away and getting outsmarted. But on the bright side, Richards stopped everything else fired at him.

With our sloppy play, we were lucky to be down by only a goal, and in the last minute, I finally had some energy that came out of nowhere. I don't know where this adrenaline came from, but I felt like I was in the prime of my career—as if I ever had a prime.

I received a saucer pass from Lawton at the red line, then burst past two forwards, quickly entering the Rochester zone. It was just me, the defenceman, and the goalie. Vaguely remembering what Lawton said on the bus about their goalie's weakness, I shot the puck past his questionable blocker side. It was in, and I just tied the game. My reward for tying it was getting hit by a Rochester defenceman. When I went down, I slammed into the boards, which made me see about a thousand stars in my head. I'm sure I got another concussion, but as long as the doctors don't make a record of it, it never happened, right?

When I got to the bench, Coach asked me if I was all right. I said, "I can play in OT."

Coach spit some chewing tobacco on the ground. "You're bullshitting me; I respect that."

He knew I was lying to him, so he decided to sit me out of overtime to keep me safe. The game ended in a shootout loss, and we were just lucky enough to get a point. Immediately after the game, we boarded the team bus, leaving the States and headed to London. Hopefully, a good night's sleep would cure these dizzy spells. When we checked into our hotel, I decided to relax and watch some TV; some old slasher movie from the early '80s was on. During a boring part, I figured it'd be a good time to break the ice with Stacy, so I looked her up and emailed her:

As you probably know, I'm back in town and tried to see you at the house, but you weren't there; I'll try again another time.

Not too much later, I couldn't keep my eyes open and fell fast asleep.

A half-hour later, my phone buzzed, waking me up. It wasn't Stacy; it was Julie, texting that Derrick scored six goals in Kitchener. I was happy for him, but I didn't feel like talking. I'd deal with her face-to-face later. Stacy didn't respond, so I assumed she wanted nothing to do with me.

It was time for our early afternoon practice, and I wouldn't have to wait long to find out if I was healthy enough to play against London. During the skate, I felt like the ice was tilted sideways—I was extremely dizzy. My balance was as bad as the local town drunk's, which would make playing hockey a billion times harder. When we went back to the locker room, I took some ear drops to help with my equilibrium, but that didn't help much.

Things didn't get much better when it was game time. Moments later, Ulf, the team trainer, let Coach know I had a concussion. This was my cue to get out of my uniform and into my street clothes. But Coach looked at me and said, "Keep your gear on. And Ulf, not a word to anyone either. Stay dressed, but you're on the bench tonight, kid."

To be clear, Coach was breaking the rules, and he knew it. But I understood why he did it. He didn't want the league to know about my concussion. Things have changed since I was a kid. Back then, hockey players had more of an invincible tough-guy image. Nobody worried about concussions. But now, that's all everyone talks about: CTE, brain injuries and the long-term risks.

But come on, I knew the risks even when I was a kid. We all did. Playing hockey means accepting that it's dangerous: you risk getting a serious injury every time you go on the ice. Not just your head, either. A single hit could leave you paralyzed—or worse, you could die.

Yeah, sometimes you get your bell rung. But this is hockey, not pickleball. Coach would likely make something up to explain why I was benched for the whole game. You're not allowed to get too many concussions in sports like hockey or football, so keeping this one off the record might extend my career by a year or two, which was all the time I probably had left anyway.

Watching the whole game from the bench gave me a better perspective of what a coach pays attention to. I wanted to play so bad, but helping Coach was more satisfying than I anticipated. I noticed London's goalie wasn't covering his left side properly, so I let the guys know. We capitalized on that weakness, scoring two quick goals to take a 2-1 lead. Then we sat back and played more conservative, trying to run out the clock.

Richards was bombarded all game, stopping 55 of the 56 shots he faced. This proved why he was an NHL-level goalie, and also why he should be back in the show. With 49 seconds left, London pulled their goalie, and they were threatening to score. A forward was screening Richards in front of the net. Not being able to play was killing me more than my dizzy spells.

With the goalie pulled, the one-man advantage gave them extra space to move the puck like a power play. One of our guys flipped it out, and I grabbed my stick, banging it on the boards. "Change!" I yelled. "I'm going on the ice!" Brown, who was dead tired, skated toward the bench, and I hopped the boards before his actual replacement could. "You better do something, kid!" Coach yelled. I knew if Coach were in my situation, he would have done the same thing. But if I screwed up... you guessed it, he'd be pissed.

With twenty seconds left, I got into the play and received a pass from Dubois. Still feeling a bit woozy, I took a shot from the neutral zone, aiming for the empty net—but I missed, resulting in an icing. With just seven seconds left, the face-off was in our zone, and London was ready to tie the game.

Coach was pissed. "Take the face-off and get us out of this mess, kid!" he yelled.

I stared down at the shaved white ice, embarrassed. He trusted me to win the face-off, something I'd done hundreds of times for him before. We skated into our zone for the draw. "Kyle, it's about time you start redeeming yourself!" Coach yelled.

With only seconds to go in the hockey game, my age and dizzy spells were not much of a factor. There's only one moment that I have to succeed in right now, and that's it: winning the face-off. It's all that mattered. There's no race to see who's the fastest or some test of strength to see who can fight; at that time, it's only between me and the other centre.

With my knees bent in a ready position to take the face-off, it was like an old Western showdown, with everyone waiting to see which gunfighter would be quicker on the draw. The ref dropped the puck, and I won it clean, sending it back to Jesse Miles, one of our defencemen. With five seconds left, Miles flipped the puck high over everyone's heads, and with a tenth of a second left, it found its way into the empty net.

We won the game 3-1. The arena horn sounded as we celebrated around Richards, while the opposing fans booed and tossed half-full beer cans at us. That was all the validation we needed. Later on, Coach told the media I had a lower-body injury, which was a good enough excuse for sitting out most of the next game—and it meant one less concussion the league knew about.

CHAPTER 11

GET DRESSED!

We lost the next game 2-1 in Hamilton and finally got back to Riverstone Bay. We got off the bus around 2 AM, and everyone went their separate ways to cabs or their own cars. All I wanted to do was confront Julie.

Richards whistled at me and said, "Let's split the cab fare!"

I had a better idea. "I'll pay the whole thing. Just drop me off at The Corner."

Richards looked at his old chained pocket watch. "Pressie, last call was about thirty minutes ago. I got some booze at the apartment."

I smiled. "Good to know, but drop me off there anyway."

The cab driver was getting impatient. "Meter's running, boys. Make up your minds."

"The Corner, please," I said, handing the cab driver a twenty.

The car pulled away, and a few minutes later, I was dropped off at The Corner.

Like a criminal plotting a bank heist, I knew each employee's every move. I also knew Julie was always one of the last to leave. A couple of servers filed out of the bar, which meant Julie was still inside, counting the night's liquor sales. I was thinking about all of this, knowing it was crazy. I was standing outside an alley where bar employees exited their workplace.

What was I doing?

Just then, the busboy and dishwasher walked out, so I knew Julie would be next to leave. The bar staff noticed me standing by, and I'm sure it looked odd to them, but it didn't bother me as much as it probably should have.

A couple of minutes later, Julie exited the bar, took a look at me, and shouted, "What's with you? I haven't heard from you in days."

I'm not exactly the smoothest talker, so I got right to the point. "So, how long were you planning on waiting to tell me that he might not be my kid?"

Julie froze as if she had been dropped into an Arctic Lake. She just stood there, silent. This was her chance to come clean, but the only sound I could hear was the buzzing of the fluorescent lights in the alley.

I raised my voice slightly. "With Connor? In my room?"

She was still in shock, but I continued, "You know what, don't even say anything. You're one less thing I have to deal with here. I'm starting to think coming back was a big mistake."

An employee, watching us like an audience member at a

junior college play, spoke up. "Is everything okay?" That was my cue to exit alley left, and get the hell out of there!

Walking back to my place, replaying events, my negative thoughts heightened. When I was in front of her, I justified my behaviour, but now I realized I wasn't thinking straight. This wasn't the first time I did something like this, yet I still hadn't learned. But still, her saying nothing in that dark alley confirmed she was flawed just like myself, Connor, Derrick and everyone else in Riverstone Bay.

We had an early practice to prepare for Winnipeg the next morning. Feeling a little better, I was still unsure if I'd be healthy enough to play later that evening. After practice, while we were taking off our smelly hockey gear, Lawton read a newspaper headline: "Winnipeg's Larson Out for Blood." The paper was referring to Blaine Larson, Cody's older brother, who was looking for me.

Lawton tossed me the article, and I gave it a look. "Great," I said. "If I don't play, he's gonna think I'm ducking him."

Where I'm from, sticking up for your family is one of the most important things someone can do. I understood what he was doing, but that didn't mean he was right. Blaine either overlooked or didn't know that his brother had come off as a dick during camp and was the one who tried to injure me.

He was only going to look at Cody's side of the story, but as many know, there are three sides to every story: their side, your side, and somewhere in the middle, the truth. So, Cody's side was the version Blaine was gonna run with.

He was going to be this heroic big brother, avenging Cody's injury. I've been there; any real family member protects their siblings. I'd done it plenty of times for Connor—the same kid who betrayed me and the same kid I accidentally killed. Blaine Larson certainly wanted me to join Connor in the afterlife that night, but I wasn't one hundred percent ready.

The sports writers didn't know I had a concussion, and the paper promoted this game like it was WrestleMania, pushing a half-truth storyline about the Cody Larson incident, glossing over Cody's attempt to injure me. The writers generated a buzz; everyone wanted to see this fight. This matchup had the same big-fight buildup as Probert-Domi II. Plenty of Winnipeg fans were in attendance, and they were loud, rude, and drunk.

When I walked into the locker room, Coach told me I wouldn't play, but that soon changed when our loose-cannon owner, Ryerson, sashayed into the dressing room. We all shut up once he entered. He looked at Coach and asked, "Why isn't he in his gear?" Ryerson stood no more than five feet from me, acting like I couldn't hear him or something.

However, our team trainer, Ulf, emphasized that I needed one more game off, just to be safe. Ryerson wasn't listening. "The Hell he's not playing! Get dressed!"

I couldn't believe this. "You're joking," I shouted.

Ryerson snapped, "No, I'm not joking! This rink is standing room only; it's not the time for a bait and switch! You're fine, get dressed!"

I felt a lot better than the London game, but if I took a shot to the head, I wasn't sure what would happen. Still, I took off my red tracksuit and got ready.

Just as the PA announcer introduced us, I quickly got dressed and joined the rest of the team on the ice. While standing there, looking up at the rafters during the anthems, I thought, *I'm playing tonight, but should I really fight?* I guess I contradicted Connor's haunted journal entry of me being 'fearless,' but I'd rather fight Larson when I was healthy.

Everyone watching the game had no clue what I was dealing with.

These blue-collar fans paid hard-earned money to be entertained. Witnessing a special moment live is something you never forget. That feeling is exactly why I fell in love with this sport in the first place. So yes, I understood them.

The game started. I wasn't on the ice, but Blaine was. He was obsessed with hurting anyone on our team, and he targeted the first person he saw: Tyler Smyth.

Honestly, Blaine should've picked on someone else—or just waited for me. Smyth grew up enduring harsh Saskatchewan winters, grazing his father's cattle. As a kid, he played hockey, wrestled his older brothers, and toughed it out in sub-zero temperatures. Fighting someone like Blaine Larson was nothing for him. Smythy knew what time it was, and they squared off right in front of our bench. Smyth got the better of Larson in the beginning, then Larson landed a few on Smyth before they both started throwing quick, short punches to the head.

The crowd was electric! Blaine got maybe a couple more in on Smyth, and then they wrestled each other to the ice. As God is my witness, I'd never heard a small hockey arena so damn loud! Both fighters skated toward their penalty boxes, but before Blaine took his resting spot, he turned to me: "I hope your gloves aren't cemented on, Prescott. I'll see you in five minutes."

This was one of those nights where they might as well have played disco music after each stoppage of play, because it was violent 1970s hockey at its finest. In today's politically correct climate, leagues often shy away from this rugged style of hockey due to negative publicity and media pressure. Ironically, some of the media helped hype this game in the first place.

Commissioners and marketers are out of touch with what real fans want. They only care about how much money they can get from sponsors and TV networks. Hockey's higher-ups need to accept that violence is part of the sport, and fans love it. Just ask the crowd that night, counting down that five-minute major as if it were New Year's at Times Square.

There were eight seconds left in the penalties, I was on the ice hovering over their blue line, right next to the boards. Lawton and Shedden were trying to set up, then Shedden passed me the puck. I fired from about 50 feet away, but Winnipeg's goalie, Marky Riddick, caught it, so the whistle blew for a stoppage of play.

At that point, the penalties were over. Blaine was back on the ice, and the crowd was going nuts—they knew what was gonna happen next. Blaine was chirping at me, and as both teams took the face-off, Smyth was beside him on the wing.

It was time.

It didn't matter if you were on the ice, on the bench, a peanut vendor in the stands, or watching the game on TV; you knew something would erupt.

The official dropped the puck, and off were Blaine's gloves, hitting the ice just as fast as the puck. Before I could accept the challenge, Smyth already answered the bell. Smyth had something to prove to himself since Larson got the better of him in round one, but this time, Smythy gave it to him pretty good, with five unanswered punches.

The crowd went insane, and the air horns blasted all over the arena. The fight was over, and I could hear a couple of Winnipeg fans yell things to me that weren't too friendly, something like, "Hey Prescott, Smyth bailed you out, you broad." Those clever remarks were very creative, but the way all of this went down wasn't what I wanted.

Smyth saved me from something I was expected to do, making it look like I couldn't fight my own battles.

Regardless, this was Blaine's second fight that he started, and he was ejected from the game. But hockey players have good memories, so I suppose there's always next time when I'd be one hundred percent.

As Blaine skated toward the visitor exit, the fans yelled everything you don't say at church while he gave them all the fingers. When he left the ice, that nostalgic '70s hockey feeling was still in effect.

Richards had a few friendly words for Blaine, shouting, "Enjoy your night off."

That got under Blaine's skin, and he body-checked Richards.

Richards went down faster than an Olympic diver, embellishing the whole thing.

When an opponent attacks a goalie, you have no choice but

to react. The rest of our guys skated toward Larson, but two linesmen got in front of us and ordered us to go to our bench.

After a few back-and-forth taunts, this scrum was over. Looking at Richards, I said, "Great acting, Richards. You can get up now."

Richards, still flat on the ice, replied, "I can?"

"Yes, Richards, get up. You look like a soccer player."

The fight card for the rest of the night ended, and an uneventful hockey game broke out, as we lost 4-2. It wouldn't be fair to put all the blame on myself for the loss, but I was on the ice when they scored all their goals. Coach didn't have much to say afterwards, but he did praise Smyth by shouting, "You can take a farm boy off the farm, but you can't take the farm boy out of Smyth!"

Even with the loss, Smyth and Lawton played incredible games. They were easily the two best players on the team, and maybe even top five in the league. Lawton had a highlight-reel goal tonight, but I saw him on his phone again, looking like he just found out his dog died or something. Whatever the case was, he looked upset, and I needed to figure out what his deal was.

He was taking his time getting changed when I tapped him on the shoulder and said, "Smythy and a few of us are going out tonight; you have no choice but to join us, rookie."

Lawton agreed to join us.

"The Corner it is," said Drexell.

"The Corner?" I said, nervously. "Nah, let's check out the Irish pub next door instead."

Richards, already dressed in his street clothes—a 1925

double-breasted suit and a fedora, interrupted us, "It's because you want to avoid Julie, isn't it?" He then invited himself to the bar with us.

CHAPTER 12

JUST PLAY HOCKEY

So, we all went out for some drinks. As we sat around a table, Smyth approached me with a couple of beers in hand. He passed me one and said, "Hey, I know how it looked with me stepping in and all, but I knew you weren't ready to go tonight."

I was relieved that I didn't have to fight, but I couldn't say that to anybody. Slowly, I took a sip of my beer and replied, "It's no problem," though it was one of those lies you tell when everyone knows it's a lie.

Then Drexell said sarcastically, "But look on the bright side—with Larson being suspended, we won't see him for a while." As Drexell, Lawton, Smyth, Richards, and I hung out, we asked the bartender to switch the TV from soccer to hockey. They turned the channel to *Sportswire's Non Stop Hockey Highlights*!

Sportswire made for much better background noise as we

debated whether to play darts or pool. All that banter came to a halt when we saw a clip of a Dallas player crash into the net and suffer a serious injury. This was no longer background noise on TV—Dallas was our parent club, which meant any one of us could get called up when they needed a body.

Sure enough, no more than twenty minutes after we watched that replay, Smyth's phone rang.

He walked outside, and we watched through the dirty pub window as Smyth grew more excited. We knew what was happening. Smyth busted back in, yelling, "I'm going to the show!"

The crowd cheered, and everyone was happy for him—except Lawton. Luckily for Rick, I was the only one who noticed his jealousy. As people congratulated Smyth, I leaned over to a dejected Lawton and said, "This isn't like you. I'm telling you, Rick, you'll get there soon enough."

"But Dallas saw something in him, not me," Lawton said as he stared at his basket of pretzels. "My parents put a lot of pressure on me. They expected me to be in the NHL by now."

At that point, I was a little bit concerned. "We all have pressure, bud," I replied. "At least you have parents; mine were basically Coach and my sister."

Just then, Richards interrupted us. "Hey, Pressie!"

"Gimme a minute, will ya?" I said, turning back to Lawton. "The billet house—is it okay?"

"Yeah, it's fine," Lawton said. "Actually, I'm glad I'm not in Michigan with my brothers and them."

"You're lucky to have family; they mean well," I said. "If I can help, I will."

Lawton looked up, holding a pretzel. "Thanks, Kyle."

"No problem," I said. "Besides, I'm the one who needs to worry."

Lawton lowered his eyebrows. "Why?"

"I lost my bodyguard," I joked as Lawton tried to hide a smile. Then I roasted him about his Michigan accent, and he snapped out of it.

Richards, still standing around us, asked, "Hey, Pressie, you hungry?"

The bar was about to close so I took one last swig of my beer and replied. "Yeah, actually, I am."

"How about pizza?"

"Only if you're buying," I said.

Richards ordered pizza on his phone. We left the pub and sprinted back home as the rain began pouring down in sheets.

In about thirty minutes or less, there was a knock at the door. Richards quickly ran from the sofa to get his holy grail of mozzarella, mushrooms, bacon, and pepperoni.

"Pizza Pizza!" Richards shouted.

Annoyed, I asked, "That's who you ordered from? Man, Pizza Pizza sucks."

"Well, now you don't get any," Richards barked. With money in hand, he finally opened the door, anticipating his Pizza of Destiny, only to be extremely disappointed. "You're not Pizza Pizza!"

It was Julie, standing in the rain. "No, I am not. I do apologize, but you should consider trying out for the diving team."

"Why would I do that? I'm a hockey player," Richards replied.

This conversation was getting on my nerves, but Julie wasn't here to critique Richards' diving skills. I made my way to the door. "She's talking about your acting when Blaine Larson took a shot at you. Now, get in here before you catch pneumonia."

Julie stood on the doorstep, being baptized by the rain. "I have a better idea," she said. "Come on."

She walked toward her car, and I quickly followed her.

"New car?" I asked.

"No, it's my mom's."

"It's very nice," I said. "Now, what do you want?"

We got in to avoid the rain. She didn't waste any time. "You played like shit tonight, and what's with you going to that Irish pub?"

I wasn't in the mood for this. "So, you came over here to insult me?"

"You're injured, aren't you?" she asked.

"I'm dealing with a few cobwebs from the Rochester game."

"I knew it," she said. "That's why you didn't fight Larson."

I scoffed. "You love getting personal with hockey players, don't you?"

Julie banged her fist on the steering wheel. "I figured I'd start with some small talk, you prick."

Just then, the pizza man pulled up, jumped out of his car with two orange boxes. This was my excuse to get out. I opened the door and said, "This conversation was stimulating, but dinner has arrived."

"Kyle, we both know you hate Pizza Pizza! Now get back in the fuckin' car!"

She wasn't wrong about me playing like shit, or how I only liked Pizza Hut. Finally, she got to the real reason she came. Julie looked up at the car ceiling and took a deep breath. "Your brother and I were in the same classes for a long time before you and I even met," she said, pausing to collect her thoughts.

I stared at her, waiting for her to continue.

"But after you came along, I thought you were the one, and I assumed Connor and I would just stay friends... But we can both admit you sucked as a boyfriend."

Oh, she walked into an iron rake with that one. "So you justify that by hooking up with my brother?"

Here we go—the part where she would list all the times she caught me messing around.

"Oh yeah Kyle? What about the two in Niagara Falls, or when I found out about the American girl, or all the other times you conveniently forgot to tell me about."

To be fair, there were a few she didn't know about, but she wasn't done.

"After all the times you cheated, I just saw you as a selfish child I couldn't trust. By the time you made the NHL... Let's get serious, Kyle."

"What about me being in the NHL? You mean the time you slept with Connor some more, then with me the day I came home? So did Stacy know about you two?"

Julie nervously ran her hand through her hair and didn't answer me. Then the conversation was about to take a detour to afternoon talk-show hell—the kind of shows I used to watch when I should've been looking for a job back in Coldwater.

"So, am I the father, or was he?" I asked.

Julie sighed. "I don't know. I figured since both of you were gone, I'd just say that you were the father."

Looking at her was impossible, so I turned away, staring at the rainwater cascading down the passenger-side window. After a few moments, I looked back at her and said, "We have to face the truth."

She took a deep breath and exhaled slowly. "Kyle, sometimes dreams don't come true. Just play hockey, and everything will work itself out."

That was enough. I got out, slammed the door, and she floored it out of the parking lot. Maybe she was right, and maybe the pizza in my apartment had already taken a savage beating from Richards, with it getting colder by the minute. I walked back inside, knowing she probably wouldn't voluntarily take the test. But she would have to—sooner or later.

CHAPTER 13

CALGARY STAMPEDE

In the meantime, our schedule was nonstop, and we were battling our way to get to a .500 record. This season, the Wranglers were finally no longer the worst team in the league, and everyone knew beating us wouldn't be easy.

As the season rolled along, the December snow dropped in to visit Riverstone Bay. A ton of snow fell, closing schools and shutting down most businesses that were still in business. Even the matinee game against Detroit was postponed due to the blizzard.

Now, with this day off, I decided to burn off the extra calories I consumed the previous night and went for a run in the snow. Wearing thick boots, sweatpants, and a heavy jacket, I searched for the deepest snow and biggest hills, looking for the earth's toughest challenge. After about forty minutes, I'd had enough and called it a day.

Maybe that was a bit too much for someone my age. On my

way back home, I passed by the old house, and the landscapers were there again, this time shovelling Stacy's sidewalk. There was an extra shovel in the truck, so I offered to help.

The landscaper, whose name I forgot, shouted from a distance, "Hey, I was at your game against Windsor the other night."

We lost that game.

"Sorry, man. You came on an off night," I replied. "Have you heard when she'll be back?"

"You missed her by a day. She won't be back until the new year," he said.

Julie's words, *Just play hockey*, repeated in my mind. Easier said than done. Another year was over, and this was going to be another depressing Christmas.

I walked back to the apartment and saw Richards watching TV in the living room. I assumed he was watching cartoons, but it was Front and Centre. They must have aired the episode early, replacing our postponed game. Most of the show focused on my interviews, and all I could think was, *Uh oh*. This wouldn't be easy to watch.

"Pressie, I can change it if you want," Richards offered.

"No, I need to see this," I said, turning off my phone to avoid any calls or texts.

The show was again very well done, but this time I didn't hate it. They used the right parts of me owning up to my actions, explaining myself, and asking for forgiveness. Seeing myself on TV, reliving the worst moment of my life, wasn't fun, but I knew I had to deal with this. Sometimes, when we face the truth, we find out that the anticipated fear we build inside is worse than the actual outcome.

The episode ended, and my phone was still off. Richards had gone to his room for a nap. Then, there was a knock on my door. I opened it to see Julie, who wasted no time pushing her way in. She wrapped her arms around me and kissed me. We made our way to my unkempt room, two bodies in lockstep, hearts pounding, and souls merging... and there's no need to explain what else happened. But when it was over, I calmly asked, "What are we gonna do now?"

She repeated what she said earlier, *Just play hockey.*

This was probably going to complicate everything outside of hockey. I was still wondering why she hadn't taken the paternity test yet. But still, what happened between us—happened.

Not that I cared, but that political snake Ryerson loved the Front and Centre episode and our improved record. He told us in a team meeting that we didn't have to take the old bus to Calgary, Saskatoon, and Sudbury. Instead, he was letting us fly in his old man's private plane. The team was excited, but I didn't care. The devil also gives you nice things, but only if you obey him—but at what cost?

Our first game was in Calgary, and we beat them 5-0. Everything went our way: the bounces off the boards, the calls from the refs, the battles in the corners, and the two fights that night. We were primed and ready to take on anyone in the league.

We were supposed to head to Saskatoon after the game, but our pilot ended up with food poisoning. So, we got to stay the night in Calgary. To make things even better, this was Drexell's hometown, and he was excited to show us a couple of night spots. He wanted some of us to meet in the hotel lobby at 10 PM. Thinking it would improve our team chemistry, I agreed to meet Drexell.

Richards, Lawton, and I all met up with him. Drexell shouted with great enthusiasm, "Welcome to Calgary! My name is Brad Drexell, and I'll be your tour guide."

We followed his lead as we stepped into a strip club. "You took us to a strip club?" I asked.

From the looks of it, cleanliness wasn't one of the bar's strong suits. Drexell laughed and proudly said, "This place is a little blue-collar, but hey, if your wallet's right, everything will be all right."

Richards quickly scanned the seedy surroundings and asked, "My wallet won't get stolen here, will it?"

Drexell laughed and turned to me with a smile. "Prescott, you might need to keep an eye on our goaltender here."

We all sat in a tattered leather booth with duct tape holding it together. There were seven or eight girls dancing; maybe three of them were halfway decent. This hole-in-the-wall place had some down-to-earth charm, though. Some might say 'down-to-earth' is just a polite way of calling something 'white trash,' but this place was somewhere in the middle—kind of like a lot of us.

There was no valet parking or overpriced cover charge here—just the scent of burnt popcorn competing with cheap body spray. On the other side of the bar, a group of bikers were playing pool, looking like they wanted any excuse for trouble, so we left them alone.

A dancer walked by our section, smiled at Richards, and kept walking. Richards, his eyes got as big as stop signs, exclaimed, "Did you see that? I think she likes me!"

Drexell looked at him with a stern face. "If you have enough money, she might love you."

Lawton turned to me. "Kyle, I really do think you should keep an eye on him tonight."

"Why do I have to?" I shouted over the Toby Keith song playing in the background.

Just then, a waitress, way better-looking than any of the dancers, walked over to our table. She wore a denim skirt so small it could've passed for rope—and was probably illegal in some of the Territories—and a matching vest that barely covered her midsection.

"Welcome back to Cowgirls, Mr. Drexell. What'll it be?" she asked.

"Welcome back?" Lawton asked.

Drexell ordered a round of Molson Export, and the waitress slowly walked off, flaunting what little clothes she had on.

Richards smiled like a four-year-old in a toy store. "I think I'm in heaven," he said.

"No," I replied. "More like a direct gateway to Hell."

Lawton chimed in, "Or chlamydia."

"Yeah, you're right," I said with a laugh.

Drexell, enjoying the moment, said, "Boys, this is what it's all about, right? The fame, the fifty dollar per diem, the... C-section scar on Mercedes over there."

"Mercedes?" Lawton laughed. "More like a dump truck."

We all laughed a lot, just hanging out and relaxing in the dive bar. In that moment, I realized this team had finally become a solid unit, and it was all thanks to times like this, bonding off the ice. The drinks were going down fast, and I had to take a whizz. As I got up, I thought, Since I'm here, I might as well enjoy myself. When I returned, I noticed Richards was gone.

"Where's Richards?" I asked.

"He found the love of his life," Drexell replied.

"How much money does he have on him?" I asked, worried, since we split the rent.

"Who knows, but the next time we see him, he won't have any left," Lawton answered.

"If he's not back in five songs, I'm getting him," I said.

Drexell lit a cigarette. "He's in good hands," he assured me, pausing for dramatic effect. "Very good hands. Technically, just one hand."

"That's fantastic," I said with a half-smile, sipping my beer.

Then all of a sudden, a buzzed Lawton stood up and made a speech. "I'd like to dedicate this night to Mr. Kyle Prescott!"

Everyone clanged their beer bottles together. Then a dancer approached me and asked if I was ready to go to the "VIP Stampede Room".

Confused, I asked, "What the hell is this?"

Drexell, the mayor of this bar, explained, "Lawton told Diamond you wanted a dance when you stepped away."

Call it peer pressure, but I gave in and went along with it.

How bad could one dance be, anyway? As I walked to the Stampede Room, I thought I recognized someone by the entrance; but since I was already a little drunk, I brushed it off.

The dancer and I settled into a small room, no larger than an outhouse at a national park. The furnishings were modest, to say the least, with one of those metal folding chairs for me to sit on while she gyrated in front of me. Not too far from where I was, I could hear Richards finishing up with whatever he was doing in his little VIP Stampede area. Meanwhile, Diamond who looked close to my age, got straight to the point and asked me what I wanted to do with her.

I really didn't want to do anything, so I said, "Actually, why don't we just talk?"

With her thick Alberta accent, she said, "You came to the Stampede Room just to talk?"

"Well, Diamond," I replied, "there's someone back home that I'm trying to work things out with."

"Where's home?" she asked.

But before I could say Riverstone Bay, I heard a loud crash in the main room, and the '90s country music stopped.

"Son of a bitch!" I yelled, quickly exiting the Stampede Room with Diamond not too far behind. What I saw next looked like a scene from an old Van Damme movie. Lawton, Drexell, and Richards were brawling with three guys from the Calgary team— and along with them was Cody Larson!

Cody moved gingerly, relying on his crutches for balance. He had this dead look in his eyes as he gave me an update on his injury. "I'm out for at least a year," he said. "And if I were you, I'd retire by the time I'm back. Hell, if I were you, I'd just shoot myself."

Though his reunion speech warmed my heart, I didn't have

time to exchange compliments. My teammates needed me before someone got thrown through a window. I quickly turned around and pulled someone off Richards, who was taking a few direct hits. Then, out of nowhere, I got smashed in the back by Cody's crutch. By the time I turned around to give Cody a receipt, it was too late—the police already showed up.

How could they have gotten here so fast? I thought. But judging by the pristine reputation of "Cowgirls", these cops had probably been here plenty of times—most likely "VIP Stampede Room" visitors themselves.

In any event, Richards, Lawton, Drexell, and I were all arrested, while the Calgary boys got away with it. The bikers who had been playing pool called the police and told them we started the whole thing, and the cops took their side. Next thing we knew, we were all in jail.

I later found out why Cody was there in the first place. He was from Calgary, and was friends with many of the guys on that team. Cell phone videos of the brawl went viral, flooding social media and the news. Coach watched the report from his hotel room, and he was pissed.

Chapter 14

Attracting Problems

We spent a couple of hours in jail, and I hoped to stay there rather than face Coach. At least the cell only smelled like disinfectant spray this time, a major improvement compared to the last time. Then, Coach finally arrived to bail us out.

Once we were all inside his hotel room, Coach let us have it. When he asked what we had to say for ourselves, I kept quiet, but Richards raised his hand like a third-grader waiting to be called on.

"Shut up, Richards!" yelled Coach.

Apparently, he didn't want to hear from us. Instead, he threw down a newspaper with a headline that read, "Wranglers Get Rowdy at Strip Club". He stared at all of us.

"Once we get to Saskatoon, there's a mandatory morning skate for everyone, even those who didn't go to the bar."

The media was all over this, newspapers were full of speculation and innuendo, and radio stations entertained the topic with misinformed radio callers blaming me. Hey, I'd been arrested before, so of course it was all my fault, right? Luckily, the video quality was poor, and there was no way Julie would have seen me leaving the Stampede Room with Diamond.

Even though I didn't do anything with her, explaining anything would only cause problems. Still, there was no denying we'd been in a place we shouldn't have been. As I thought about the price of getting nice things from Ryerson, I remembered a Bible verse from an old man in Coldwater: "What good is it for someone to gain the whole world, yet forfeit their soul?" (Mark 8:36).

That verse shook me up. I was still falling for the same traps I used to fall for when I was a rookie. The embarrassment was bad enough, but we also got fined and suspended for the remainder of the road trip.

Richards, Lawton, Drexell, and I were given black practice uniforms the second we walked into practice. Black uniforms only meant one thing—black aces. I'm not sure where the term comes from, but the meaning was clear. Anyone wearing all black in a regular-season practice would not play in the next game— NO EXCEPTIONS!

The whole team stayed silent as we dressed, except for *les boys de Québec*—Dubois and the others—talking under their breath, *"Pourquoi on n'a pas été invités?"* It wasn't like we were headed to the electric chair, but then again, this morning's skate was going to last longer than getting electrocuted.

The clock's red digits indicated it was 7:02 AM. I turned my head and saw Coach already on the ice, standing there, pissed. We all skated up to him.

"Good morning boys. Now, some of you guys wanted to go to a brothel that's a front for a pool hall!" Coach yelled.

Drexell quietly stated, "Wouldn't it be a pool hall that's a front for a brothel?"

Luckily, Coach didn't hear that, and he continued his tirade without missing a beat.

"Only a handful of you were there, but as a team, you're all being punished. At the sound of my whistle, start doing laps."

He blew his whistle, and we were off, skating for what seemed like a year. Then the next time I looked at the clock—it only read 7:07. We had only been on the ice for five minutes, and I already felt like I was going to die. I'm sure we all did. A shift in hockey lasts about forty-five to sixty seconds. No matter how fit you are, you still need to catch your breath and rest.

But there was no rest in these opening moments of torture. Coach sent the guilty and not guilty straight to frozen Hell. We were all breathing heavily, and my legs—probably felt like everyone else's—like they were on fire, and heavier than tree trunks. Finally, Coach blew his whistle after a few more minutes, telling us to get some water. Coach began another speech.

"I know how you four like to have fun, so let's continue the fun!"

The next drill was called *the gauntlet*. Richards, Lawton, Drexell, and I stood by the sideboards while everyone else got to hit us. They all got up early because of us, so they took out their frustration with every hit, knee, and elbow. After a few minutes, Coach blew the whistle and told us to get off the ice.

That night, when we played Saskatoon, it was a certified beating. We were out—checked, out—hustled, and outclassed. Our backup goalie, Haywood, hadn't played in a while, and he looked terrible. We lost 8-0, and then we lost the next two games. By the time our suspensions were over, we had lost three more in a row.

I had a day off and decided to go for a walk to clear my head. But just as I stepped out, my phone rang—it was Ryerson.

"You need to be in my office in ten minutes," he said, and then he hung up.

When I entered Ryerson's office, he was sitting behind his desk, remote in hand, flipping through channels. He landed on *The Steve Santos Show*, where the host was loudly blaming me for the stampede incident and shouting that our season was over. Ryerson turned his head from the screen for a moment, then switched off the TV.

"Are you really going to believe Steve Santos?" I asked.

Ryerson replied, "Doesn't matter if I believe it or not. We both know that a lot of people believe whatever TV says. Do I think this is your fault? No. But you were there, which makes it a story."

This was my moment to say something that needed to be said. "You wanted me here for a story in the first place, and now I guess it's backfiring."

Ryerson leaned back in his stupid gamer chair and said, "It's not backfiring. We're going to use this to our advantage." He wanted to exploit the media for exploiting us. He wanted to see a verbal confrontation between me and Steve Santos live coast-to-coast.

Leaving his office, I realized once again, I had to face the firing squad. I thought, I'm just a giant magnet attracting problems—one after another with hockey, Stacy, Julie, Derrick, and Connor. After the meeting with Ryerson, I knew I needed some serious soul-searching.

I walked into the cemetery, feeling Connor's presence. It was like he was expecting me this time. My anger from his betrayal slowly slipped away. Yeah, what he did hurt, but there was no question about who the real bad guy was. As I approached Connor's headstone, I felt something telling me I was being too hard on myself. I don't know if it was God, Connor, or my own voice, but I knew the guilt I'd carried all these years wasn't healthy. A voice behind me said, "You know he's forgiven you, right?" It was Stacy's voice.

I turned and saw her for the first time since the funeral. She still looked fit, but a little weathered from the pain she endured. I was speechless for a moment. There was a weak tone in my voice when I finally said, "I can only hope he has. Have you?" Like a coward, I stared down at the snow.

Stacy took my trembling hands. "Kyle, I know the guilt has been a burden on you, and it's been a burden on me too." She continued, "I should've known what you two were up to that day. It was my job to protect both of you."

Her words broke my heart, but it wasn't her fault—it was mine.

"I'm the one who decided to drive, not you, I would've found a way to take that car, no matter what."

Facing this fear and finally seeing her was when the healing began. I told her, "I can't fix what I broke, but I'm here to salvage whatever I possibly can."

Stacy wiped tears from her eyes and said, "Just do one thing." She paused, meeting my eyes. "Make me and your brother proud." This was the moment I'd waited for almost half my life. We embraced, releasing years of pain in the presence of our brother.

This moment should've happened a long time ago, but maybe this was the right time and place for it to actually happen.

Before we parted, Stacy told me I was always welcome at home. With a smile, I asked, "I am?" She quietly laughed. "Yes, just use the front door this time—don't break in.

CHAPTER 15

SHOWTIME

The stage was set for my appearance on The Steve Santos Show. A black luxury SUV pulled up to my apartment building's parking lot, and my phone rang. It was Ryerson's assistant, Dale Palmer.

"Car service has arrived," he said. Still not ready to leave, I tried to buy some time. "You guys are early; I still have to get dressed."

Dale calmly responded, "That's all been taken care of. We're actually running late; come on."

I left my place and got into the vehicle. "Where's Ryerson?" I asked. Dale, furiously typing on his phone in the front seat, replied, "The boss was supposed to ride with us, but he has an important meeting today."

I wasn't going to ask Dale what Colton's meeting was about; I figured it was either a court date or a date with an escort.

Besides, I had bigger problems. A red suit hung from a dry cleaner hook in the backseat. "They expect me to wear that?"

Dale put away his phone. "Well, yeah, it's the style," he said.

I took a good look at the red blazer, which looked purposely too tight, and the matching red slacks, and laughed. "There's no way—give Deion Sanders his suit back."

"We have plenty of time to discuss fashion before we get on set," Dale said, handing me some note cards.

I flipped through them quickly. "Looks great," I said, deciding it wasn't worth arguing about. I already had a good idea of what I wanted to say to Steve Santos, and I knew it would be better than Dale's bullshit responses.

Arguing with Dale would lead to him texting Ryerson, so I let it slide. When we arrived at the studio, I'd be live on television in less than thirty minutes. When it was time to get dressed, I lied, saying the suit didn't fit right through the shoulders. Instead, I would wear blue jeans, a flannel shirt, and tan work boots.

The set had a typical sports talk show look, with LED screens and neon lights flashing "Steve Santos" behind us. His techno music played, and the stage lights went from dark to bright, revealing Santos, a coffee table, and me in the middle of the set.

As the theme music faded, Santos introduced me. "Some know him as the dude who captivated this country as a teenager, scoring the game-winning goal in the World Junior Championship many, many years ago, but to me, he's the guy who bailed on his hometown. He's the same dude, he's Kyle Prescott, and he's live on The Steve Santos Show!

Santos began. "Kyle, I wasn't sure how you'd feel about being on the show,"

I wasn't thrilled, but I tried to keep my cool. "I'm not sure recording this show live is a good idea, Steve."

"Sure it is! It's great to have you here, Kyle!" Santos replied.

Dale tried to get my attention backstage by flapping his arms and gesturing for me to read the note cards, but I ignored him. "Oh yeah, it's good to be here," I said. "Now you can look me in the eye and repeat all that shit you've been saying about me and my team for the last two weeks."

Santos looked shocked. The show's theme music abruptly played, forcing a commercial break.

As we went off-air, I turned to Santos. "What the hell was that?" I asked.

Arrogant as ever, Santos pointed at the neon lights. "You see that?" he yelled. "That's my name—Steve F'n Santos. This is my show! My set! Stick to the script!"

Before I could respond, the techno music started again, and a headset-wearing crew member counted us down. Once we were back on air, Santos demanded to know my side of the story about being arrested in Calgary.

I leaned forward. "You think you've got it all figured out?" I asked. "Just because I was at the bar, it's all my fault? Then you've been running your mouth nonstop since. I was in the wrong place at the wrong time—kinda like you are now. If you want to keep taking cheap shots at me or my town, we're gonna have some problems."

There was dead silence. Santos wasn't a big guy, but still, he was a bully, surrounding himself with employees too scared to tell him what they really thought of him.

But I say what I want, when I want to. When talkers like Santos get called out, they'll insult you or resort to violence. But since he'd probably never been in a fight, he decided to insult me:

He asked me a probing question, "So, Kyle, what was your favourite meal in jail?"

I'd warned him, but this was the fun part.

I said, "I miss the Jell-O they gave us." Then, in the politest manner, I flipped the coffee table between us, shoving him backward onto the floor. About five people with headsets rushed in to make sure things didn't get any worse.

Dale quickly guided me out of the studio and back into the SUV. The driver was already inside, and it was time to leave.

Dale's phone rang—it was Ryerson. Dale turned to me and said, "I'm putting this on speaker so you can hear how much trouble you're in!"

Dale answered nervously, "Colton, I know what you're thinking, and I can assure you we provided the red suit to Mr. Prescott."

"Screw the red suit!" Ryerson slurred. "That was amazing! It couldn't have gone any better!"

Women's laughter was heard in the background.

Dale quickly replied, "Oh, I agree—it was actually my idea!"

Ryerson, taking a deep breath, said, "I don't care whose idea it was. I loved it! Now we just have to spin this to make Santos look like the asshole—which won't be hard since he's live on-air firing off F-bombs!"

"When should we start?" Dale asked.

"We?" Ryerson replied. "That's your job. I might be tied up with this important meeting for another day or two." Women's laughter continued in the background until Colton Ryerson hung up.

"Oh boy, Dale, it sure sounds like I'm in big trouble," I said, laughing.

Dale shrugged, relieved. "Well, I'll just make a tweet later."

CHAPTER 16

FAMILIES MATTER

The snow had melted, and after my appearances on Front and Centre and The Steve Santos Show, the town rallied behind us. The Wranglers were back to our pre-stampede winning habits. We beat Detroit 7-2 in the makeup game postponed by the winter storm. The dated arena was now consistently sold out with a kinetic energy that was contagious.

The people of Riverstone Bay, who lived and died with our wins and losses, clearly connected with us. This was evident in the city centre, which transformed into a sea of red and black—our team's colours—as huge banners of our team concealed the abandoned buildings.

A team photo, which included me, now hung inside The Corner, further evidence of the town's unity. But we still had to shake the stigma of being a drinking town with a hockey problem. The next day, we had to battle against some familiar opponents—Blaine Larson and the Winnipeg Warlords—which was definitely going to be a serious hockey problem.

Our inconsistent play throughout the year meant we still needed two more points to make the postseason. A deep playoff run would make us a lock for National Hockey Day, but first, we had to qualify.

Coach could feel the pressure—Hell, we all could—and missing the playoffs was not what anyone in town wanted. After a great practice, I was heading back to my apartment when Julie texted me, asking me to meet her at the rink in four hours. I knew Derrick had a game against Brampton to advance in the OFSAA playoffs, but something told me I needed to be there for more than just the game.

When I arrived, I couldn't find Julie. As I scanned the crowded stands, my phone buzzed. It was a text from her: Hey, I'm stuck at work, so you're gonna must keep me updated until I get to the game.

Since she never asked me what happened in Calgary, I gladly gave her the highlights. However, I was sure she didn't want to hear that they were losing 2-0. Derrick hadn't been playing well in the first two periods.

Right when the third period started, my phone buzzed again: Marco finally showed up for his shift. What's the score now?

I replied, Same as before; still down 2-0 in the third.

She didn't respond, but soon enough, she showed up, doing her shouting and micromanaging routine from the stands. She gripped her usual hot chocolate and started interrogating me.

"They shouldn't be down to two goals. Why haven't they scored?"

She was losing it. *Yeah, I'd like to see you do better*, I thought, but I didn't say that. She knew hockey, but watching from the stands gives you perspective players don't have on the ice. A player doesn't see the big picture like you would see if you were watching on TV. Derrick got off the bench and looked right at us. "Just let him play," I yelled to Julie, trying to compete with the loud arena noise.

She stood there, clutching her hot chocolate in her right hand. "Well, I guess there's only so much I can do, but it's those two," she said, pointing at the two girls Derrick partied with.

"What are you going to do right now? Attack them and get arrested? Julie, please, just watch the game."

There was still plenty of time left for them to come back, and sure enough, Derrick scored. "About time you got your head on straight!" Julie yelled.

He didn't have a dumb celebration after he scored—he probably knew Julie had already found out about his earlier performance. He tried hard to tie the game, and they came close when his team pulled the goalie, but Brampton scored an empty-netter, putting an end to their OFSAA Championship dreams.

The final buzzer sounded, and we watched from the stands as Derrick's team sat on the bench, defeated. "He got off to a slow start," I said. Then, I tried to be funny: "But once you got here, he played better to avoid your yelling."

Julie didn't think that was funny, even though it kinda was.

"Where is he?" Julie asked. "I don't see him on the bench or the ice."

"He probably stormed off to the dressing room after the last goal," I said.

Julie shifted her eyes to the two girls Derrick partied with. A guy, who looked about twenty, was with them. The three made their way out of the arena.

"Did you see those three?" she asked. "Come on, Kyle, follow them."

They were too far ahead, and there were too many people between us to catch up. I had a feeling Derrick had already changed into his street clothes and would leave with them. A few minutes passed before we finally exited the arena. Julie trotted toward the SUV.

I was right: Derrick had already changed and was inside the car with them. The SUV sped off. Julie and I exchanged a worried look.

We got into her car and followed them, keeping them under surveillance from a distance, but soon, we were stuck behind a slow car that stopped at a stale yellow light. As we both impatiently waited for the light to turn green, we tried to guess where they were headed, and at the same time, we both said, "Overtime!" A place famous for serving minors.

As the light finally turned green, we spotted the blue Ford Edge already parked at the dive.

"I can't believe they still have their liquor licence!" Julie said.

I fired back, "Did they ever have one?"

Julie gave me a look and told me to shut up—the kind of look that said I'd be sleeping on the couch if we lived together.

We parked and rushed inside the run-down teen club. The interior design consisted of chain-linked fences, stolen road signs, traffic lights, and posters of rock bands taped to a brick wall. Derrick and his friends were surrounded by drinks, and the haze of pot smoke cut through the flashing lights. The dance floor, a cracked concrete slab, was where the two girls Derrick knew danced seductively to modern rap music blasting from the blown-out speakers.

Seeing Derrick in this party element was like watching an old VHS tape of myself, making the same mistakes. I was in a daze, haunted by the similarities in how he looked and carried himself. Julie snapped me out of it, yelling: "Are you gonna help me with your son, or are you just gonna stand there looking stupid?" Derrick gave us a dirty look, visibly embarrassed, and quickly busted his way past us, leaving with his friends.

His defiance was his mask; he wore it to hide his vulnerability through the guise of teenage rebellion. We followed Derrick outside to the blue SUV as I grabbed the twenty-year-old's keys.

"Where do you think you're going?" I asked. He looked soberish, but we weren't taking any chances. Derrick and his older friend kept quiet as Julie turned to the two girls Derrick had been hanging with. "I don't like either of you," she said coldly. Then, turning to the older guy with them, she added, "And I probably won't like you either."

I stepped in. "Do us a favour and get the hell out of here." I tossed the keys back to the twenty-something guy. They sped off, kicking up gravel in the unpaved parking lot. As they drove away, they mustered the courage from the safety of their car to flip us off and shout insults. Julie's earlier comment finally sunk in—the one about Derrick being my son. In my mind, I heard that famous talk show host shouting,

Kyle Prescott, you ARE the father! I was glad I was, but whether I was his dad or not, it didn't matter... Derrick needed me. On the drive back to Julie's mom's place, things were quiet for a minute, but I decided to break the ice by talking about the game.

Slowly, everyone started to cool off. When we pulled into the long dirt driveway and parked, the garage still had plenty of room. I noticed a hockey net inside. This was the perfect moment to really talk to Derrick. Julie gave me an endearing look, nodding at me, and she went inside. Derrick was headed the same way, but I stopped him.

"Got a left-handed stick lying around?" I asked.

"Yeah, we got one," Derrick replied.

My voice shook a little as I asked, "Wanna take some shots in the garage?"

Derrick shrugged. "Since my plans changed tonight, and now that I don't have anything better to do, sure."

We grabbed sticks inside the garage and started passing the hard orange hockey ball. Derrick asked, "So, how was playing in the show?"

"It went by so fast, the show was cancelled before I knew what hit me." A memory of the semi-truck hitting my car flashed in my mind. "I made bad decisions, and I paid for them, Derrick.

Some of those decisions were the same mistakes you made today." I took a shot, hitting the crossbar.

Derrick got the rebound and passed the ball back to me. "Yeah, well, there's always tomorrow."

"Believe me, Derrick. There's no guarantee of that."

He changed the subject. "Why'd it take you so long to come back?"

I was about to fire another shot, but in mid-windup, I stopped, and put down my stick; I owed him my full attention. "I guess I wasn't ready for all of it, and that wasn't fair to you. I can't make up for the time I was gone, but from this point on and until I die, I swear to God, I'll do whatever I can to be the best father that you can possibly have."

Julie walked outside, interrupting us. "Derrick, don't you have homework?"

Derrick took one more shot; the orange ball flew under the top right corner. He put away his stick and quietly headed inside. Before going in, he turned around. "Good luck tomorrow, Dad."

Julie walked up to me and gave me a hug, and I thought, No, I couldn't fix what I broke, but salvaging whatever I could was starting to look realistic.

Before returning to my place, I decided to grab something to eat at The Corner. When I walked in, I was warmly greeted by the employees and patrons with words of encouragement. I couldn't help but notice the changes since I arrived here last fall—not just the decorations outside or the photo of myself in there, but the attitude of the people. They had a glow to them, something that didn't exist seven months prior.

They understood that I was just like them, no matter if I once had a million dollars or if I was broke—at this point, I was much closer to being broke than a millionaire. The server asked if I was going with my usual, a Reuben with a beer on tap, and I nodded.

"Actually, I changed my mind. I'll still have the sandwich, but I'll have a water."

"Got it, a Reuben and water coming right up." The server walked off.

Just then, *The Steve Santos Show* played on the TV.

Santos set the scene for tomorrow night's game against Winnipeg, predicting that we would lose and not make the play-offs. His rationale behind his little prophecy was based on a couple of factors. First, Tyler Smyth was no longer on our team, having played so well for Dallas that he never returned to our club.

Second, Garret Marshall, the player Dallas traded away, had resurfaced in Winnipeg. So now, he was our problem along with Blaine Larson's blood thirst for me.

Santos continued to poke fun at our team, showing high-lights of how Winnipeg had soundly beaten us in the last game. He even threw in a couple of clips of the mistakes I made on the ice, pushing the narrative that I was washed up and that this should be my final game.

My first step towards sobriety started with some confusion.

The server returned with a bottle of water. "Oh no," I clari-fied, "I meant a glass of ice water—the free kind." The server walked away with the water bottle, and Santos continued his so-called expert analysis. "But let's not kid ourselves, guys. Prescott can say he's back playing hockey to right the wrongs or for the love of the game all he wants, but we all know he's just doing it because he needs the money."

That bothered me.

But since I'm not allowed on The Steve Santos Set after our little disagreement, there wasn't much I could do about it—except shut him up tomorrow night. The server brought my free water, and I asked if he could change the channel.

He switched it to the local news, which was covering a live report about a blue Ford that had collided with a train. Derrick's friends were inside—the three he planned to party with that night. The twenty-year-old driver was hospitalized with a serious head injury. His new criminal record would be the least of his concerns; he'd never be the same. This would be a wake-up call for Derrick. He could now use this, along with my past, as inspiration to clean up his reckless behaviour.

CHAPTER 17

THE WINNIPEG WARLORDS

The time had finally come, and the weather outside was unseasonably hot for early spring. A mob of wild Wrangler fans crowded around the players' entrance, with police and security fighting to hold them back. Our fans were everywhere—you'd think it was a championship game.

The rink had separate entrances for each team to get inside, but I was close enough to the Winnipeg area to make a few observations. I spotted Blaine Larson and Garret Marshall arriving just as Sean, one of the regulars from The Corner, started shouting at the Winnipeg players.

"Hey, Blaine, how's little Cody holding up?" Sean taunted.

Larson gave him a nasty look and replied, "Just for that, I have something special for your hometown loser. After I send him to the retirement home, you'll need therapy—though it seems like you're already getting some!"

Sean stepped closer, challenging Larson. But even Blaine wasn't dumb enough to fight a drunk fan in front of police and security, so the bully resorted to an insult.

"Better fire that therapist and find someone more qualified to help you get over the beating you're about to witness."

Sean moved closer, likely hoping for a pull-apart from the cops, who eventually stepped in to hold him back. Once Sean knew it was safe, he shouted, "Hey, I heard Smyth gave you a sex change, buddy!"

The crowd erupted, everyone laughing at Larson.

On our side of the segregated entrance, we all laughed too, passing the cop cars and security to enter while our fans cheered and wished us luck.

Inside, the heat affected the ice conditions, casting fog across the ice surface and giving a dramatic, final act feel to the environment. It would impact both teams equally but added an unpredictable element to the game.

Moments before the game, Coach walked into the locker room and stood silently, his emerald eyes piercing through all of us like a needle through a pincushion. For thirty seconds, he said nothing, and none of us dared to say anything to piss him off, not even Richards. Then, he began one of his speeches.

"This whole season, Winnipeg bullied and embarrassed us. Trust me, boys, that's exactly their plan tonight—to do it again. We all know how important this game is, and with the pressure we're under, there's a lot of uncertainty. But there's one thing for sure: we have to play like our lives depend on it."

Coach paused, letting his 1986 movie speech hit home. "This

game isn't just about two points. We're playing for everyone in this town, and we all know that."

The arena horn sounded, indicating it was time to get on the ice. The rock music of Accept's Teutonic Terror blasted through the walls as Coach finished, "Play like your lives depend on it. Because it does!"

That was it. That was the mindset we all had as a team. We got up and headed toward the foggy ice, the fans cheering as we stepped onto the surface. The game started, and we had to communicate more than usual to set up plays because of the increasing fog.

We moved the puck into the Winnipeg zone, but lost control. Winnipeg gained possession, and a winger passed it back to a defenceman. Jesse Miles pinched in deep and slammed him into the boards, rattling the old glass. The crowd exploded as if it was the greatest thing they'd ever seen. He got the puck and passed it to Lawton, who scored. Just like that, we were up 1-0.

Winnipeg won the face-off and dumped the puck into our zone. Richards went to play it behind the net when Garret Marshall decided to goon it up, hitting Richards and sending him to the ice. At first, I thought Richards was trying to sell another injury, like before, but this time, he was legitimately hurt. Marshall was given a game misconduct for the hit; however, that wasn't much consolation since the team trainers had to work on Richards.

When we saw our backup goalie, Ryan Haywood, putting on his mask and doing warm-up stretches, we realized Richards wasn't coming back. Only forty seconds had passed, and our NHL-level goalie was already out of the game.

Coach was absolutely pissed! He looked at us and shouted, "Richards is gone because you let them take him out! Now it's time to protect each other and hurt these bums before they can hurt you! Are you going to let some criminal break into your house and let them take everything right in front of your family? You've got your family here tonight! Winnipeg is trying to rob all of us in front of our loved ones! Dammit, this is our house!"

Coach spat his chewing tobacco, looked at Haywood, and said, "You're ready for this. I know you are."

But was Haywood ready? He was a little inconsistent, and he let in too many bad goals, like the eight in Saskatoon. Coach put me on the ice. As I stepped on the ice I took a look towards the stands, I spotted Julie and Derrick—five rows from the glass—cheering loudly alongside the buzzing crowd.

I knew Derrick, Julie, and Coach were all expecting something from me—something to set the tone for tonight's game.

As a defenceman, my job was obvious: to defend! I was supposed to stop the opponents from getting a scoring chance. If I couldn't trust Haywood, then no one was getting a shot on net.

The puck dropped, Lawton won the face-off, and it came back to me. I didn't do anything spectacular; I just bounced it off the boards for Drexell to take down the ice. However, he couldn't get a good handle on the puck, and Winnipeg gained control, coming toward us.

I transitioned from skating forward to backward. Three Winnipeg forwards raced toward me and my defensive partner,

Dubois. Their centre passed to the right winger. I lined him up perfectly and slammed him into the boards, rattling the old arena's glass once again.

The crowd cheered even louder than the times we scored. I passed the puck up to Lawton, and I knew he was going to do something special. He skated past both defenders and made their goalie look clueless as he put the puck right under the bar, making that sweet, dull sound of iron.

We were up 2-0. The crowd lost their minds. With every game Lawton played, it became clearer he was ready for the NHL. I was just happy to help, like I promised him the night Smyth got called up. About thirty seconds later, my shift was over.

I went to the bench to grab some water, but within ten seconds, Winnipeg's Brady Roberts scored to make it 2-1. It was their first shot on Haywood, and it went in. You couldn't help but think the worst. Thirty seconds later, he scored for a second time. Just like that, it was tied 2-2. Then, on the same shift, Roberts scored again!

Coach grabbed my sweater and said, "From now on, you're on the ice whenever he is. But first, get rid of Larson."

Coach put me out there as a winger, right next to Larson. We said a few words, then the puck dropped, and so did the gloves.

It was time.

Finally, I was battling Cody's big, bad brother, Blaine Larson.

Blaine took a swing, so I lowered my head. His right hand hit the top of my skull, and I'm pretty sure he broke his hand because he switched to his left. Then he popped me in the nose, tears exited my eyes and blood poured out like a volcano erupting.

But Blaine stepped over his own stick and lost his balance. I saw my chance and started swinging. I hit him with everything I had—all the frustration from every setback since my brother's accident and remembering the Coldwater war cry of getting back up, taking chances, succeeding, failing, and trying again—My lips went numb, and I took it all out on Larson. I can barely remember the fight, but our blue-collar fans will.

It was over in less than forty seconds. The trainers needed to check Blaine's hand, and it was indeed broken, so he was done for the rest of the game. I'm sure I'll see Blaine and Cody again soon, but, luckily, for the time being, the Larsons were not a problem that night.

Even though we could do the 1977 goon stuff as well as anyone, we just wanted to play hockey and beat them. The rest of the game was tough, but nobody was trying to hurt anyone anymore. Despite being down by a goal, we'd established our authority and had the crowd on our side.

When it was the second period, we were still losing. Then I had a chance to tie the game. Their goalie, Riddick, was out of position, and I had a wide-open net. But sometimes your mind plays tricks on you when it's too easy. I shot the puck over the net. The whole crowd sighed in disbelief. My insides sank like I'd just gone down a roller coaster.

I sat on the bench, embarrassed about my mistake. Then, out of nowhere, Coach asked if I was ready to keep up with Roberts —their best player who had scored all their goals. Out of breath, I said, "Coach, I don't know."

Coach responded with something I wasn't ready for. "Yeah, I don't know either. Let's do it anyway."

That was his motivational speech—probably the worst speech he'd ever given me. So, not only was I playing my shift as a defenceman, but I was also supposed to jump on the ice the second Roberts did. The only way I could get through this was to lie to myself and say I could do it. And you know what? My lies worked. Roberts couldn't get a shot on goal when I was shadowing him.

But once their coach saw what we were doing, he switched the lines so Roberts stayed on longer, even during my defensive shifts. This caused confusion with our line changes, and we almost got called for too many men on the ice. I could barely breathe after being out there for two and a half shifts.

Then, Roberts's fresh legs flew past me in the neutral zone. He received a pass from his defenceman and was on the verge of a breakaway. Somehow, I caught up, but I had to trip him, resulting in a two-minute penalty. It wasn't the worst decision either. Roberts had Haywood shell-shocked, and there was no doubt he would've scored again. Sometimes, you have to take a penalty to get by. Whether or not it would backfire, we'd find out soon enough.

There was 1:53 left in the second period, and we had to survive my penalty.

During the five-on-four penalty kill, the boys played it safe, dumping the puck and making Winnipeg chase it. After about thirty seconds, Roberts was tired and left the ice. But there was still time on the penalty as the PA announcer said, "One minute remaining in the second period."

As I sat in the penalty box, exhausted from shadowing Roberts, I watched the seconds tick away. I questioned how I'd missed that easy scoring chance earlier and even wondered why I should keep playing this game. I thought about all the athletes I idolized and how a lot of them played a year or two too long— slow and not putting up big numbers anymore. As I was feeling sorry for myself, Winnipeg got into our zone and started passing beautifully.

"Twenty seconds left." I was standing in my plastic and plexiglass cage, watching the play develop. Then I noticed they were going to pass to their defenceman.

"Watch the point man!" I yelled.

Lawton must have heard me because he intercepted the pass and skated with the puck, their defenceman close behind. "Ten seconds left." I'm not taking credit for Lawton's breakaway, but maybe I am.

Lawton had just enough time to score, but he was hauled to the ice, and the puck slid into the boards. We all expected a penalty shot, but the referee swung his arm backward, signaling a two-minute tripping penalty. No penalty shot. The crowd was furious, and Coach was pissed!

The period ended, and we headed to the locker room. By the end of the second, we had 43 shots on goal to their 36, but we were still down by a goal. We were tired—especially me—but Coach reassured us that Winnipeg was running out of steam too.

He spoke with a cold, calculated tone that gave us the confidence we didn't have earlier in the season.

The third period was a fast-paced, back-and-forth thriller. Both goalies were standing on their heads, stopping everything in sight. I kept shadowing Roberts, frustrating him into mistakes. I was proving that older players could still contribute, even if we weren't scoring 50 goals a season. But I knew I still needed to score. I had to make up for missing that wide-open net.

The rest of the period saw both teams have great chances, but we kept missing by inches. Drexell hit the post, and the puck ended up on Roberts' stick. He had another breakaway, but I chased him down, distracting him enough to make him put a weak shot on Haywood. Haywood, to his credit, had redeemed himself. He was playing as well as—Richards! I didn't keep my promise to prevent shots on goal, but now we could trust our backup goalie.

Time was melting away faster than a snow cone in Phoenix, and with only fifty-nine seconds left, Coach pulled Haywood for an extra skater. The face-off was deep in the Winnipeg zone, but they controlled the puck and quickly broke out. After a few passes across the ice, they were about twenty feet away from scoring an empty-net goal.

Everyone thought it was over. The score would be 4-2, and our season would be done. But somehow, their shot attempt failed; they missed the net! I quickly grabbed the puck and passed it to Lawton. He knew exactly what to do. With Drexell on his side and me trailing behind, we entered Winnipeg's zone with enough time for one last chance. "Twenty two seconds left!"

Lawton blasted the puck so fast, none of us even saw it. We thought it was in, but it wasn't—it was caught by Riddick.

There were only sixteen seconds left.

Coach called a timeout, and he told me to do something I didn't agree with. He wanted me to be the centre and deliberately lose the face-off, putting the puck on one of their defenceman's sticks. It sounded crazy, but both of their defenceman on the ice were known for being clumsy.

As I glided towards the face-off, I looked into the stands and saw Stacy making her way down the steps to join Julie and Derrick, but there was no time to process that.

Here we go, I thought, bloody sweater, little time, my hometown watching. Let's go.

The puck dropped. I lost the face-off, just as planned, and skated toward the defenceman who had the puck. I stole it and fired a wild shot, bouncing the puck off the back of Riddick's pad —and it went in! The game was tied, and we were going into overtime. *Holy shit, it actually worked!* I thought.

The crowd roared, and my teammates tackled me in celebration. We acted like we had just won the championship, even though we weren't even in the playoffs yet!

We headed to the locker room with huge smiles—drying off the sweat and preparing for overtime. Colton Ryerson, walked in with a few words of encouragement. He told us how proud he was and that we were winners no matter what happened. It was strange coming from him—either he had turned a new leaf, or he was on something.

But then he told Coach to check his phone. Coach reached

into his pocket, checked his phone, and put it away. He said, "Boys, we've got a game to win."

We walked out of the locker room, each of us getting a pat on the shoulder from Ryerson as we headed back onto the ice. Half the crowd was cheering for us. Then more of the arena was cheering and losing their minds, hugging each other in the stands like they just watched us become champions. We stood there, not ready, wondering what they were doing.

Then the puck dropped, and overtime ended abruptly as Roberts scored ten seconds in. Our season was over. As far as I was concerned, so was my hockey career. When you lose in overtime, the first thing you want to do is get off the ice as soon as possible.

But not that night.

The arena was still giving us a loud ovation that lasted several more minutes. You don't often see a sold-out crowd giving a standing ovation for a team that just missed the playoffs, but there it was. When we acknowledged our fans by tapping our sticks, I looked toward Julie, Stacy, and Derrick, all celebrating together! Seeing all three of them united as a family was the perfect moment. But it took me a few minutes to fully understand why our crowd wouldn't stop cheering.

All of us in that old hockey arena took the loss together; our playoff hopes had crashed and burned, but our town's dreams still rose from the ashes. Just before the start of the third period, Colton Ryerson had received a phone call that changed our town. National Hockey Day was indeed coming here. He couldn't contain himself and quickly posted the news on social media.

By the time the game went into overtime, many fans had discovered the news, and word spread quickly. Ryerson, the con man, had intentionally withheld it from us before overtime, unsure how it would affect our gameplay. Ultimately, it didn't matter.

That spoiled brat made his father proud and played a key part in our town's comeback. It's not like he transformed into a saint, but maybe he wasn't as bad as we all thought. We've all made a few mistakes—or a few million. What really matters is if you can redeem yourself after a failure or not. I realized some don't get a second chance, but a few of us in Riverstone Bay were lucky enough to get one.

CHAPTER 18

THE GHOSTS OF THE OLYMPIA AND MAPLE LEAF GARDENS

Ice sculptures glistened in the sun like a dream. Families of all ages tied their skates and rushed to the frozen pond as excitement radiated through the crisp winter air. The festivities were in full effect, with jazz music serving as an upbeat soundtrack, mixed with the town's familiar voices and laughter. This was it; National Hockey Day was here, injecting new life into Riverstone Bay. The comic book shop, the arcade, and the hardware store—once just memories—finally resurrected, smiling at me with a fresh coat of paint. But even more exciting news was yet to be announced.

The jazz musicians ended their performance when Colton Ryerson jogged up to the stage.

"Weren't they great!" Ryerson began, gesturing to the musicians with his game-show-host swagger. The crowd of thousands, including nearly the entire town, stood by the stage, impatient, eyes glued to their phones, rolling their eyes. Among the chatter, you could hear people saying things like, "He's probably up there to give himself an award."

Someone else jumped in. "Yeah or one of those giant checks."

After the microphone feedback faded, Ryerson looked out at us and began, "Alright now, I'm not up here to put a spotlight on me. I'm here today to put it on this town and its people."

The crowd grew quiet, and several people, witnessing Colton Ryerson's honesty—maybe for the first time—looked away from their Galaxy or iPhone screens. He cleared his throat and continued:

"As many of you know, our town has been through a lot. We were wounded and abandoned. Half of our gift shops and restaurants went out of business, leaving former owners with more questions than answers. Many struggled to afford food and other living essentials—let alone a ticket to watch a losing hockey team."

Ryerson took a breath and continued, "With everything this town has faced, I admit I couldn't relate to those struggling. For too long, all that mattered was me and my needs. Deep down, I knew I had serious problems and made mistakes."

He paused, looking directly at his father. "You all resented me, and so did my dad—and I deserved it. My selfish actions nearly cost me everything, and I became a little desperate. One day, I watched old hockey highlights of Kyle Prescott, a Riverstone Bay kid who was expected to be one of the very best. But life had other plans, and he indeed lost everything. I'll admit, signing Kyle was a publicity stunt, but once he arrived, he kept fighting—for himself and for all of you—and that's a fact. Day by day, he checked every box necessary to for him to become a man." Ryerson turned to me, his voice full of pride. "Kyle, we're all proud of you. Now it's time for you to do the honours, bud."

The crowd gave a loud ovation. Ryerson then exited the stage.

Now it was my turn. I've been through worse—how hard could a speech be, right? I took my time walking up the icy wooden steps to the stage, wondering if what I was about to say would work—especially since Connor was about to speak with me. As I got closer to the podium, I recognized many faces in the crowd, young and old, from Riverstone Bay and even Coldwater. I spotted the rink manager, Kent, and the little Tim-Bits accompanied by their parents. All of them were a big reason this happened, and I was positive they realized that.

So I walked across the stage, and as I looked at the sea of people staring at me, I began to panic, but I reminded myself that I wasn't doing this alone—not this time, not anymore. After a couple of moments of silence, I could tell the crowd was becoming restless—or maybe that was just me overthinking everything. Regardless, thousands were waiting for me to share a few words about this unique, historic occasion.

So I breathed in the cold February air, looked at a beat-up spiral notebook, and began reading the words written by my brother several years ago.

OCTOBER 25TH, 2005

The ice we play on is the canvas for the artwork we are creating. The ghosts of the Olympia and Maple Leaf

Gardens are whispering to each other, and they do not like what they're seeing. They don't like to see this once-pure game become a corporate business.

I looked directly at Colton Ryerson and smiled as I said that. Colton smirked back, giving a light clap in acknowledgment of the tiny jab. It felt surreal, like my brother was right there with me, helping me give this speech. I looked down at the pages and continued:

The game has become more a business than the foundation it was built on. Hockey was built on Bobby Baun's broken leg, scoring the game winner in the 1964 finals'. The game exemplified perseverance, when Gordie Howe came back from a life-threatening head injury in 1950. Historic events that gave hope to millions, like Paul Henderson in 1972, and Mike Eruzione in 1980. These deserving men persevered through times so diffi-cult, so unrealistic, yet they still stood tall, immortalized.

That was the last thing Connor ever wrote in that notebook, so I picked up where he left off. Gently setting the notebook on the podium, I addressed the crowd:

"The ghosts didn't think about quarter-billion-dollar TV contracts when they first laced up their skates. They didn't play in front of flashy CGI board ads or care about big sponsorships; the game was raw, with the soul of local communities.

Simply put, today's game is just a business trying to catch up to the other three sports. The ghosts also didn't consider wearing special uniforms with political statements when they skated on a pond playing for no money.

They understood sacrifices: Kids leaving family to live with strangers to play in a more competitive league. Sacrifices and selfless acts summed it up perfectly. Connor didn't seek attention; he just wanted to play hockey.

When he didn't want to play, his selfless act of letting me take his World Junior spot made me realize how fortunate I was to have Connor, not just as my best friend, but more importantly, my brother.

We all know that he isn't around to accomplish his dreams because of me. Still, Connor's presence, legacy and memory made this moment possible. If you have the chance to make things right, do it; redeem yourself. That's what both of us tried to do."

Then, wiping a tear from my eye, I proudly stated, "At this moment, I have the honour to announce that we're standing on the future construction site of the Connor Prescott Memorial Auditorium."

My words came from a place that was real, but some buried truths will remain hidden beneath the surface. I wanted to preserve the illusion of Connor's perfection, so I chose to be the gatekeeper, concealing a detail or two about him.

When I stepped away from the podium, Coach Johnston was waiting. I gave him a big hug. He looked at me, tears in his eyes, and said, "You did alright, kid." As we let go, he added something I wasn't ready for: "No, you did great, man." If it weren't for Coach, I might have still been an overgrown child with little purpose, and Connor could have just been some trivia question on a coffee cup.

Sometimes dreams do come true.

Words can't explain the feeling in that moment. The crowd was freezing but still cheering. Coming of age usually doesn't take this long, but for me, it did. Like I said before, this was the exact place and time for it to happen—all of it. Everything I went through—no, everything we went through.

Then, Julie came up to me, kissed me, and told me she'd always loved me. Yes, she made mistakes, but she had her reasons, yet, she was forgiven. Next, Derrick and Stacy appeared. Stacy, with her white figure skates draped over her shoulder, embraced me and said, "Yes, you made me and your brother proud."

I turned and saw the landscaper Mitch Landon standing there with a smile on his face. He was sharing a hot chocolate with his daughter, who looked to be about five years old.

"Mitch?" I paused, feeling overwhelmed. "I'm glad you made it." Mitch shook my hand, and I smiled at his daughter. I knelt down to her level and said, "Hey! Tell your dad he still has a couple tickets waiting at will call."

Then, out of nowhere, Richards appeared, looking like he'd looted a sporting goods store, holding four pairs of rental skates. He smiled and asked, "Hey Pressie, do you think it's safe to go on the ice?"

"Is it ever safe for you, Richards?"

Julie laughed and yelled, "Shut up, Kyle!"

Then, all of us found a bench to tie our skates, and I soaked in this winter celebration throughout Riverstone Bay. The sounds of kids laughing, shouts of excitement, and the slicing of skates across the ice could be heard a mile away. This was the greatest moment of my life. I was no longer living in the past, holding onto accomplishments from nearly two decades ago.

Once again, I was living in the moment, looking forward to my future with my family. Finally, I could let go of my past because the redemption of Kyle Prescott had come to fruition. Now it's up to us, as a family, to define how we want the Prescott name to be remembered. What does that mean? Maybe I have a season or two left in me, and hopefully, Derrick has about twenty to go. If so, then I can tell a few more stories about the legacy of the Prescott family.

THE END